Fainting Goats
as Pets

Fainting Goat / Myotonic Goats

Owner's Manual

by

Ludwig Lorrick

Contents

Introduction 6

Chapter 1: The Fainting Goat 9

Chapter 2: History of Fainting Goats 13

Chapter 3: Summary of Fainting Goat Traits 15

Chapter 4: Things You Must Know About Goats as Pets...........16

Chapter 5: Why Choose Goats as Pets?.........................23

1. Raising goats for dairy 23

2. Raising goats for meat 23

3. Raising goats for fibre and fabric............................... 24

4. Raising goats for fun 25

5. Raising goats for breeding and selling 26

6. The additional benefits of raising goats..................... 26

Chapter 6: Where Do You Get Goats?.........................32

1. Traditional goat breeds... 32

2. Age considerations for goats 34

3. Adult goats... 37

4. Where to buy goats... 38

Chapter 7: Making A Home For Your Goats 44

1. Preparing the family.. 44

2. The initial days 46

3. Introducing a goat to an existing herd....................... 47

4. Introducing your goats to pets 52

Table of Contents

5. The final checklist 54

Chapter 8: Housing Your Fainting Goats **56**

1. Building the perfect shelter for your goats 57

2. Budget shelter options 59

3. Creating the perfect ambience 61

4. Bedding options for Goats 64

5. Keeping predators at bay 65

6. Fencing options 67

Chapter 9: Goat Care Essentials **69**

1. Feeding goats 69

2. Grooming your goat 78

3. Clipping goat hair 80

4. Trimming the hooves 81

5. The daily care checklist 83

6. Seasonal care for goats 84

7. Putting a pet to rest 88

Chapter 10: Interacting With Your Goats **91**

1. Understanding goat behavior 91

2. Getting goats to behave well 95

3. Training your goat 97

4. Disbudding a goat 100

Chapter 11: Identifying and Transporting Goats **103**

1. Identifying your goats 103

2. Containers you may use for transportation 104

3. Transportation choices 105

Table of Contents

4. Safety Regulations 108

Chapter 12: Breeding, Kidding and Milking **109**

1. Preparing your goats for breeding 109

2. The ABC of goat breeding 110

3. Complications during pregnancy.. 112

4. How to prepare for kidding 114

5. Is your goat ready for kidding? 116

6. Dealing with labor.. 117

7. Caring for the mother and kid.. 119

8. Care for a goat that is nursing 121

9. Creating a milking routine.. 121

Chapter 13: Health And Well Being.. **124**

1. Common diseases in goats... 125

2. Abortive Diseases.. 134

3. Parasites.. 136

4. Common vaccinations for goats... 139

5. Finding a Good Goat Veterinarian 141

6. Guidelines to Help Prevent Disease.................................... 142

7. Getting Insurance.. 144

Conclusion **147**

Introduction

If you are seriously considering having goats as pets, then you must prepare yourself for a great deal of responsibility that is about to come your way. Of course, goats are really gentle and quite cute, really! They make wonderful pets and can be really rewarding farm animals, too.

However, the most important thing that you need to understand when you are bringing home a pet goat is that this animal needs special care and attention. Yes, the regular pets like cats and dogs need the same amount of care. However, the advantage that you have with these conventional pets is that you have enough support and also a lot of information available about the health and care of these animals.

As for goats, they are seldom found in the urban set up. They are usually raised in large numbers on farms and also in designated commercial set ups where there is ample professional help available to take care of these animals. If you are planning to bring a goat home, on the other hand, you must invest a lot more time doing your homework and research about this animal in the first place. You must be sure that you can take on this responsibility before you make a commitment.

You see, the goat is a large animal. This means that you need to have enough space in your home to begin with. It is definitely not possible, and even unethical to cram a goat up in a tiny apartment. They need exercise and a lot of space in order to remain healthy.

You may choose to keep your goat in your backyard or even in a designated space outdoors. Once you do that, you need to worry about keeping them fenced and protected. If you are keeping a goat in an urban set up, the last thing you want is your pet goat breaking free and running out into the freeway.

When you bring a goat home, you must be prepared to let it stay true to its instincts. If you find a goat cute, that's alright. However, if you expect your goat to cuddle up and sleep in the same bed with you, it is time for you to consider other options for a pet. Your goat will not fetch the morning newspaper or sit on the couch while you watch TV either! It is an "outdoor" pet. This is a very important thing you need to tell yourself several times before you bring home a goat.

Now, if you are willing to let the goat be a goat, you need to progress on to the next step. The kind of food and the care that your goat needs is pretty different from the conventional pet. They have specific requirements that help them stay healthy. We will discuss that in more detail. However, what you must understand is that clean drinking water and the right kind of food is extremely essential for your goat's health.

Does a goat need more attention than other pets? Yes! These animals depict certain behaviour patterns that may require a good deal of attention, at least in the beginning. For instance, a goat needs to relieve itself a lot more than other pets. While training the goat could be possible, the time you need to spend is a lot more than a cat or a dog.

Although it may seem like having a goat is nothing but trouble, let me tell you that if you are really a "goat type" of person, this animal can be extremely rewarding! You can find a great companion in a goat! They are extremely docile creatures and are quite entertaining when they are in a herd. They will interact with you, head butt you when you don't pay attention and even follow you around if they are fond of you. The kids are extremely adorable. Watching them progress from simply stumbling to prancing around your yard is the best thing you can experience.

As for the commercial side to having goats, you can benefit a lot from breeding goats if you know how to do it right. If you have a rare breed that you want to breed and multiply in numbers, you can learn the art or seek assistance from professionals.

The next thing is showing your goats. There are several pet shows that have a special category for farm animals like goats. If you are interested in exhibiting your pet, you will have a lot to do from the word GO. You need to groom and take very good care of your goat.

Of course, on a larger scale, goat's milk is a good business venture. However that requires a good deal of investment. In any case, you can have access to fresh goat milk for your entire family, for sure!

Of course, not everyone needs to be an "expert" at goat keeping. But, you need to be prepared with all the information that you need. This book covers all the subjects including how to choose a suitable breed, how to take care of the goat, how to feed them and even how to ensure that they are always healthy. If you are a first time goat owner, this is the perfect book for you.

Chapter 1: The Fainting Goat

The Tenessee Fainting Goat is known by several other names. It is called the Stiff Leg Goat, the Myotonic Goat, the Scared Goat or the Nervous Goat. A particular behavior pattern is responsible for the different names of this particular breed.

When this goat is in shock or is surprised, all the muscles become completely stiff for about 10 seconds. The legs become especially stiff! Because of this physical reaction, the goat just falls over or appears to "faint" dramatically! This peculiar condition is an inherited one and has no real repurcussions. It is just natural for this breed.

Source: www.wikipedia.org

This is a medium sized breed. The head and the facial features in the goat are very distinct. They have a condition called myotonia congenita that is genetically inherited. Because of this trait, the muscle mass increased overall. So, the body conformation is also quite distinct with this breed.

When you purchase a fainting goat kid, the muscle mass must appear increased. This mass becomes more pronounced and prominent when the goat matures. As for the body structure, the fainting goat must appear stocky and tall. The body is wide and shows heavy muscles all over. It is also full and deep. While these are just general characteristics that you can look out for, there are certain breed standards that are important for you to know when you are bringing home a Tenessee Fainting Goat.

With these standards, you can check if you are indeed getting the right breed or if you are being cheated by a dubious breeder.

Fainting Goat Breed Standards

Here are the recommended standards for a Fainting Goat:

Head: The head should have a straight profile. The size of the head is between short and medium in length. The head does not have a convex shape or the roman nose as seen in breeds like the Boer and the Nubian.

Nose: The nose is flat and wide in appearance. The muzzle is usually broad and is rounded slightly. The jaws of this breed should have an even bite and must be full. The forehead of this breed is broad and the orbit of the eye is quite prominent. In fact, it protrudes a lot more than the other breeds of goats. This type of eye orbit is called pop eyed or bug eyed.

Usually, the head is distinct from the face region because of an evident dip that is present at eye level. The ears of the fainting goat are medium sized, both in length and width. Usually it falls horizontally from the sides of the head. Half way along the length, you can see an evident dip in the ear where it bends further down. It is common to have horned and polled animals.

The Coat: The texture of the coat varies, and so does the length. It is possible to have a coat that is smooth and long, or just shaggy. In some goats, you can see a bit of skirting around the legs. This happens even if the rest of the body has short fur. During the winter months, it is possible that these goats will grow some cashmere to stay warm. If you see fur that hangs in the form of curled ringlets, it is a defect. It does not cause health problems. However, it is not accepted for exhibitions.

Color: Originally, these goats were found only in black and white. At least, that is what the documentation says. Today, of course, with breeders open to experimenting with this breed, several coat colors have emerged. There are also many markings and coat patterns that are accepted today. Even though black and white are still most common, there is no color scheme that is rejected. Combinations of colors are most preferred.

Neck: The neck must have good muscle mass. It must seem rounder and fuller than other goat breeds. In case of the females, the neckline is more slender while the males should have a muscular and strong looking neckline. In case of many male goats, the neckline is wrinkled and thick.

Chest and Forelimbs: Like most of the other body parts, even the neck must appear muscular. When viewed from the side, it should have a properly defined angulation. The forelimbs must look tightly fixed to the body. This means that the point where the shoulder begins should be just behind the most anterior part of the breast bone. The legs should come down straight from the shoulder. The joints must appear broad and strong. The bone density should appear high from the structure of the legs. The chest of the Fainting Goat is moderately wide.

Rear Limbs: The rear limbs should have a decent angulation when seen from the side. It should not appear too straight. The legs should be placed moderately apart. They should not appear too cow hocked. As for the pasterns, they must appear straight, short and strong. The rear limbs must have a decent bone density with good muscling all over.

Rump: The rump should not be too straight or too steep. It is medium in length. The tail must appear symmetrical and must be narrow at the tip. The tail is carried over the back. The hips must reveal the dairy character of this breed. The pin bones are present lower that the hip and are quite wide and pronounced. The thurls of the goat are placed wide apart. There should be prominent muscling all over.

Back and Barrel: The back must look strong and broad. The muscularity of the back is extremely important. The ribs must be sprung well, giving enough space for the abdomen and chest. The body must be full and deep.

Feet: The feet must be proportional to the size of the goat. It must be well shaped, even and strong. The hooves also need to be completely symmetrical and should have decent heel depth.

The Skin and Hair: The skin of the goat should be clear and resilient. The coat mist be shiny. Remember, you can determine the health of your animal from the appearance of the skin and coat.

The Mammary System: The udder is quite large in size. It should not be pendulous. The texture of the udder must be smooth and firm without any scar tissue or lumps. The attachment at the rear should be high and symmetrical. In the front, it must blend into the body without any pocket.

Buck Reproductive System: The testicles should be equal in size and must be firm. There are two teats that are non-functional in the males.

These are the standard characteristics that you must look out for when you are choosing a Fainting Goat.

Chapter 2: History of Fainting Goats

The Fainting Goat or the Myotonic Goat is recognised as a distinct American breed. The origin of this breed is rather obscure, not to mention interesting.

In the 1870's a farm worker made his way to Marshall County Tennessee. His name was John Tinsley. He just showed up one day at the farm of Dr. H Mayberry. Now, this John was quite a queer man. He wore a hat that looked like a beret and spoke in a unique accent. Many believed that he could have been from Nova Scotia.

This man had with him a buck and four does that belonged to a strain that was never seen before. He simple sold these animals to Dr. Mayberry and left the farm. This, dear reader, is the best possible account of the origin of the Fainting Goat!

These goats had a very unique quality about them. Unlike other regular farm goats that were popular back then, these goats did not climb over the fence and escape. They were also extremely muscular in appearance. But, what made them really popular was their ability to reproduce. They had a very high rate of reproduction. Thus, the number of Fainting Goats began to increase.

Around the 1950s, a couple of Tennessee Fainting Goats were transported to central Texas. Here, the goats gained popularity for the quality of meat that they were able to produce. These rather large goats were given the name of " Wooden Leg" goats in these parts.

It was in the 1980s that both the Texan and the Tennessee strains of the Fainting Goats were rediscovered. People became more enthusiastic about keeping this breed in their farms. In this era, there were two distinct interest groups that emerged. One group of breeders worked the traditional way and focused on improving the meat quality of the animal. These breeders chose the goats based on the physical conformation, the growth rate and the ability to reproduce. The next group wanted to promote this breed as a unique one and opted for the smaller goats that were prone to more stiffness.

The best thing about this breed, even today, is its versatility. The breed is available in every color that is recognised among goats. Most breeders claim that the kidding season is the best as the kids can come in various colors, sometimes even new colors that haven't been seen before.

This type of cross breeding does prove that the Tennessee Fainting Goat has great genetic value. However, what is important to note is that using purebred does extensively can threaten the chances of survival for this breed. As a result, this breed is recognised as a high conservation breed.

Chapter 3: Summary of Fainting Goat Traits

Size: Medium Size 50 to 175 pounds or 20 to 45 kilos

Varieties Recognised: Mostly Black and White. All the other colors and patterns are recognised.

Status: Recovering

Purpose: Domestic, Commercial and Show

Temperament: Docile and friendly

Hardiness: Can manage heat and cold. Very hardy breed. The comb is vulnerable to frostbites.

Sexual Maturity: 4 to 6 months

Breeding season: fall

No. of offspring: one or twins

These are just a few characteristics that are unique to the Tennessee Fainting Goat. However, the breed standards have been discussed in detail in the previous chapters.

Chapter 4: Things You Must Know About Goats as Pets

Keeping a goat at home, as exciting as it sounds, is a big deal! These are not your regular pets and are very different in terms of their needs and their behaviour.

For many people, keeping goats at home involves a very significant commercial purpose. They probably want to start a business of selling goat milk and cheese. In such cases, they have extensive knowledge about raising these animals.

On the other hand, if you want to keep pet goats at home, you need to start from scratch and gather as much information as you can about the animals and then venture into the commitment of keeping a goat.

Let us just compare a regular pet like a cat or a dog with a goat. Have you ever heard of anyone trying to milk a dog? Sounds bizarre right? However, if you do have goats at home, you need to know what to do when these animals start lactating. You see, there can be serious repercussions of not milking does when needed.

We will talk about this in greater detail. To begin with, you must really know if you want to take up the responsibility of this unique animal, in the first place. There is a basic checklist that you need to go through before you bring a goat home.

I would advise every first time owner to give serious thought to the points I have mentioned below. Make sure you don't just assume that something works for you. Bringing goats home is serious business and you need to be fully convinced that you are capable of handling them.

First Time Goat Owner's Checklist

Can you even have a goat on your property?

Of course, this is the first thing that you need to check. You see, just having the consent of your landlord or even the fact that you have your own place, is not good enough for you to have a goat on your property.

Several urban areas may be permitting people to have hens and smaller farm fowl in their backyards. However, it is a different story with goats. They are larger animals and require a special ordinance to keep them in the backyard.

If you have any doubts about this, you can speak to your local council for assistance. In case there is nothing that is officially clarified, you can still seek permission from them to legally have goats in your neighborhood.

The next thing you must do is ask for permission from your neighbors. They must be ok with this. Some people may resort to complaining about you to the authorities if they are not pleased with the idea of having goats for neighbors. A few others may even try to harm your goats or just intimidate them. God forbid that you have such neighbors and the poor goat damages their property ever so slightly! On the other hand, if you have friendly neighbors who are also keen on having goats, it is great. Then, even if your local authorities are not compliant, you can get a petition forwarded to them. If they find that your petition is valid and that you can give your goat good living conditions, they may grant you permission!

You must get a license

Whether you are in the USA or UK, it is important to have a license and registration for your goat. You will have a local cattle association such as the American Dairy Goat Association where you can fill up a form with details such as the breed, gender and age of your goat.

Once the application is completed, you will receive an identification number that will be used to tattoo the animal as well for further reasons. We will discuss identification of your animal in the following breed.

Goats are not loners!

In most parts of my book, and in most other manuals for rearing goats, you will notice that the authors repeatedly refer to the goats in plural. This is because, it is never a good idea to have a single goat in your backyard! You see goats are herd animals. They have a social structure that they need to follow in order to feel content and comfortable in the space that they are living in. In case your backyard cannot accommodate at least two goats, I suggest that you reconsider the plan of bringing home a goat.

Goats can become aggressive and may develop behavioural issues along with serious health issues if they are not in the company of other goats.

Now, let us assume that you have enough space to house two goats, the next thing you need to ask yourself is whether you can afford two goats. Remember, it is twice the care, twice the attention, twice the feeding and twice the expenses if you plan to have a pair of goats in your home. So, think this through completely and speak to the other members of your family before you take that step and actually get into the demanding job of being a goat parent!

Buying intact bucks isn't the best idea

When they are little kids, it doesn't matter whether your pet is a buck or doe. The real problems begin when your goat becomes sexually mature! This is when you really need to watch out!

You see, bucks become really aggressive when they are in heat. They can also smell very bad and can be dangerous to you and people who come to your property. This is when annoyed neighbors and even the pleasant ones will find enough reason to get your goats right out of the vicinity.

There are instances when young goats have targeted the legs of their owners. They actually ram into you and can injure you. It can be really painful even when they do not have any horns. So, you can imagine how hazardous they can be to children.

So, it is best that you bring home a spayed or neutered buck. Unless you have plans of building the herd in your farm, it is recommended that you have your buck neutered before they reach their sexual maturity. These bucks are called wethers. They are really calm and docile and are a treat to have at home.

Another thing that you need to keep in mind is that your goats need to be neutered at the right time; just before they hit puberty. They also need to be checked regularly. If they are neutered when they are too old, there is a chance that they develop urinary calculi. This is more predominant in bucks that have been neutered too early.

So, the best thing to do is just bring home a buck that has already been neutered. If you just want to have goats as pets, it is the best thing you can do. There is no need to feel guilty or unhappy about doing this. If you are not able to take your goat to the breeder at the right time for mating, you could be damaging the health of your pet. So, the wise thing to do would be to just have him neutered.

Can you keep them confined

There is an old saying about keeping goats and fences. It says, " If it can't hold water in, it can't hold the goat in." I tried really hard to understand what this saying meant for a long time until I began to meet with urban goat owners who presumed that a rail fence was good enough to hold the goats in.

Goats love a challenge! They will do anything to break out. They will jump over, slide under or even head butt their way out of the "strong fence" that you believe runs around your home. If you are someone who is comfortable with a 3" cyclone fence, I have news for you. Your goat can just prance over it. Yes, he doesn't even have to take a high jump!

We will talk about housing and fencing the goats in detail in the following chapters. However, I did bring it up soon to tell you that the expenses of having a goat includes preparations like putting up a newer, stronger fence.

You must also be very careful with the type of fence that you choose. You want nothing that the goat can stick its head through and get stuck. If you have goat kids, you must be particularly careful, as they love to go and get stuck in the fences.

You must also know what type of fencing is really allowed in your neighbourhood. The electric fences that are usually used to keep farm animals in might be prohibited in some neighborhoods. Even a woven wire fence may require special permission in certain areas.

You need lots of space

The goat is essentially an outdoor animal. More importantly, it is a rather large outdoor animal. It needs its share of exercise and fresh air. If you live in an apartment, I hope you are considering moving out when you bring home your goats. Goats can get really miserable when they are confined to spaces inside your home. They may even get really sick, not eat that well and just be everything but themselves when they are kept locked indoors.

You see, goats are definitely getting used to the urban set up as a species. They are quite alright despite the noisy streets and the number of people that they encounter on a daily basis. But, what they really need to be in their comfort zone is the assurance of a large enough space where they can hide or run off from threats. As the owner, it is actually a wrong thing to do if you do not have enough space for your goats in your back yard.

If you really want to have a goat in your home despite the space constraints, ask yourself another question. How do you expect your goats to get any exercise if they can't run and walk around?

So, there should be a large enough backyard for two goats to run around and have a good time. Then, you can definitely consider having a goat as a pet.

How will you take care of your goat's health?

Goats require a lot of attention in terms of their health needs. They are more prone to parasites than most other farm animals. Goats tend to graze around when they are bored, and for food, of course. This makes them prone to several infections. It is also possible that your goat may feed on dewy grass that makes the possibility of catching an infection higher. Of course, you cannot monitor the goats all the time.

However, in case of a medical emergency, do you know how to deal with it? The biggest problem with goats is that you cannot simply take them to a regular veterinarian. There are special vets who deal with large animals like goats. So, when you do make a commitment to your goat, you also need to look for a doctor who is equipped to treat your animal.

The next thing you need to worry about is the proximity of this doctor to your home. Will you be able to take the goat to the doctor easily? More importantly, will the doctor visit your home to treat the goat when required? If you need to take your goat to the vet, you need to worry about the mode of transport you will use to take the goat to the vet.

Can you handle goat behavior?

Have you ever heard of the word capricious? It basically means whimsical or rather erratic in behaviour. While goats are fun loving and calm for the most part, there are times when you cannot really predict their behavior.

Also, the way your goat behaves depends largely on you. Yes, there are significant changes in the goat's behaviour when he reaches puberty or when he is well into the mating season. When it comes to the does, they are quite a handful when they are about to give birth. This is a natural cycle that you can expect from the goats.

However, if you spend enough time socializing the goats and allowing them to be around people more since they were kids, chances are that they will behave a lot better even when they are undergoing trying times biologically.

On the other hand, if your goats are left in the backyard by themselves, interacting with you only when you go up to feed them or change the water, then, you can expect a sort of distance in the way the animal deals with most people.

Of course, the behaviour of your goat will be significantly different from any other pet that you may have. So, you must study a little more about goat behaviour before you bring one home. We will discuss in a little more detail about goat behavior in the next few chapters to help you prepare for your pet goat.

I have no intentions of sounding negative or discouraging. However, these are some of the real challenges that you will face when you bring home goats. If you are already having second thoughts, you may want to discuss this with your family or with other goat owners before taking the next step.

Chapter 5: Why Choose Goats as Pets?

Now that you have decided to bring home goats and keep them as pets, you need to be clear about the reason why you are keeping goats in the first place. There are a few advantages of knowing the purpose of goat keeping well in advance. They are:

- You will know what breed to pick
- You will be able to prepare better for the breed that you are bringing home
- You will also know exactly what to expect from your goat in terms of financial gains. You will also be able to work out your finances accordingly.
- You can be better prepared for the common health hazards with these goat breeds.

The benefits of raising a herd of goats are many. However, before you get into the benefits, let me tell you about the basic reasons why people keep goats as pets:

1. Raising goats for dairy

The milk provided by goats is considered to be extremely nutritious. Goat cheese is often a very lucrative business for most people who bring home goats for milking. There are certain breeds that are extremely popular if you are interested in a lucrative milking business. The recommended breeds are La Manca, Nubian Goat, Alpine Goat, Oberhasli, Sable and Nigerian Dwarf Goats.

2. Raising goats for meat

For those who are looking for a pet goat, the idea of raising a goat for meat may seem downright cruel. However, it is a fact that raising goats for meat has proved to be one of the most lucrative business options for several goat owners across the globe. When you are raising goats for meat, the obvious requirements are a decent size or the breed and a certain quality of meat that the goat must be able to provide. The most recommended breeds for meat are the Tennessee Goats, the Spanish Goats and the Kiko goats.

Meat production

If you are raising a herd for meat production, you may obtain the meat either by sending the selected herd to the slaughter house directly or through livestock markets.

In the livestock markets, you may exchange the herd for another breed or a younger herd or for cash. From there, they are sent to the production unit.

Whether you are going directly or through a market, your herd requires an FCI or a Food Chain Information This is a legal requirement that lists the health details of your herd. The objective of the FCI is to ensure the quality and the safety of the meat that you are providing.

You can obtain an FCI declaration from websites of food standard agencies in your country or from abattoirs. Even your local agriculture department will be able to help you with this.

3. Raising goats for fibre and fabric

Some goats are raised especially for their fur. The fibre from these goats can be used to make warm clothing and several other fabrics.

The goats that are used for fibre or fabric are usually quite fancy to look at. They have long and flowing strands of fur. The hair may also come in several layers that differ in texture and even the purpose. Basically, you will recognise a fibre or fabric goat by the sheer exotic appearance of the breed.

Since these goats look so fancy, they also double as great show animals. It is true that other breeds are also eligible for exhibiting and for shows. However, with the goats that have exquisite hair and appearance, you will also feel like a real show goat owner, if you know what I mean.

The only concern with these breeds is that they require a lot of care and effort. Since they have really long hair, you have to take extra care to make sure that it does not get matted and soiled and appear unsuitable for use. If you are taking these goats for exhibiting, especially, the time that you spend on grooming the goats is quite a lot.

Some of the best breeds for fibre and fabric are the Angora Goats and the Cashmere Goats.

4. Raising goats for fun

Of course, there are many people out there who just find great company in their goat pets. Goats are rather gentle creatures, getting extremely aggressive only when they are on the verge of puberty or when they are in the breeding season. Otherwise, they are quite calm and will seldom attack you, unless they feel really threatened by your presence.

If you are looking for pet goats, some goat owners recommend bottled babies, or goats that have been fed using feeding bottles. Although, in my opinion, raising a goat from the time it is a doeling or a buckling and letting it be around people is good enough, there are some owners who vouch for the fact that bottle babies are calmer and much more comfortable around human beings.

If you are able to find a healthy bottle baby, you may always try to keep them in your home and check for yourself. The only issue you can expect with bottled babies is unstable health if they have not been given enough nutrition in their growing years.

Are goats really that great as pets? Yes, they can be rewarding pets. They can get attached to their owner to a great degree and may follow you around when they are kids. Even if the goats in your home do not get that attached to you, you can be assured of one thing. They can be extremely entertaining. Their quirky personality, especially the dramatic ones like the Tennessee Fainting Goat, can leave you guffawing!

The best breeds to have as pets are the Fainting Goats and the Pygmy Goats.

5. Raising goats for breeding and selling

One of the most lucrative professions with any livestock is breeding and selling. This means that you will have to gain expertise on producing larger and healthier herds in order to sell them to prospective goat lovers.

With breeding and selling, there are some pre requisites:

- You need to have a facility that is large enough to house your herd as it grows in size.
- You need to have access to professional medical assistance when required
- You should have enough experience with raising various goat breeds.

Unless you are sure about handling goats and providing them with proper care, you must not think about breeding goats in your backyard. You must be sure that the health of the breed will not be compromised upon at any cost.

If you are looking at creating and experimenting with new breeds, you must have enough knowledge and experience. You have professionals who can help you learn more about breeding goats and using compatible strains to produce newer breeds.

6. The additional benefits of raising goats

Considering that goats have been domesticated for close to 9000 years, it is not hard to believe that there must have been several benefits of raising goats as pets.

By now, you must be familiar with the several methods of running a lucrative business keeping goats. However, besides the monetary benefits, there are several other reasons why you must consider keeping goats at home:

1. You can be more self sufficient

A successful and lucrative business with goat products can be expected only when you have a sizable herd. If you are planning to own goats for business, you may plan the size of the herd as well. However, you can experience several personal benefits by keeping even two goats at home. Having a goat at home can really make you self-sufficient.

To begin with, your dairy expenses will be automatically reduced if you have goats at home. If you purchase recommended dairy breeds, you can have enough milk for you and your family, without any hassle.

You may argue that it is difficult to keep caring for pregnant goats and therefore, milk may not be a product that you can expect from pet goats. However, the truth is that your goat needs to have one delivery of kids for you to start milking it. Following the first delivery, you can obtain milk for almost 3 years without re-breeding! This is the average time span that has been recorded by several goat owners. However, the duration may be shorter or longer depending upon the breed that you have at home. The milk can be converted into great quality cheese as well!

Second, you can have access to fabric and fibre if you have a breed like the Angola Goat at home. The hair from this breed can be used to make blankets, sweaters and other products. If you take the hair to spinners, they can make several other products for you as well.

You can get the best fibre from goats. You must have herd of Cashmere shawls. They are made from Cashmere Goats. Breeds like the Angora and Pygora produce Mohair. Then, when these two breeds are crossed, they produce another type of fiber called the Cashgora which is extremely popular across the globe!

2. Automatic weed control

If you are distressed about the perpetual weed cover in your backyard, you might want to consider having a pair of goats in your backyard. Everybody knows that goats are great weed removers. They can keep your garden and backyard free from all sorts of weeds.

It will be interesting for you to note that several goat owners actually rent their pets out to their neighbors and friends to clean the weed in the backyards and gardens. So, you have another mini income source right there for your goat!

In fact, when people have larger goat herds, cities and certain municipalities also hire them to keep the area free from weeds. In areas that are overgrown with weeds, goats can be quite the helping hand. They are great even when you have to clear out blackberry bushes.

These goats are usually leash trained and are handled on the leash to ensure that they don't just take away all the flora from a certain patch of land. So, if you are used to taking your goats on walks using the leash, here is another way you can exercise and feed your goat!

Goats are preferred as weed removers for several reasons. Some of them are:

- You can reduce the use of chemical herbicides
- The quality of the soil improves with time
- The diversity of plants will improve with removal of weeds
- Weeds can be removed in areas that are hard to reach. For instance, on steep hills or in denser areas of plant growth.

So, you see, your goat's ability to eat almost all kinds of foliage is actually a blessing in disguise. If you are worried about your goats eating poisonous plants, you can be pretty sure that the goat has instincts about what it may eat and what it may not. However, to help you keep your goat away from deadly plants, I have provided a list of potentially hazardous plants in the following chapters. You need to know how you can identify these plants to keep your goats safe.

3. Goats for child and youth engagement

There is a certain youth group called the 4H that basically aims at helping youths reach their highest potential by aiding their development. This group is administered by the National Institute of Food and Agriculture of the United States Department of Agriculture (USDA).

Of the several engagement activities that this group conducts, interacting with animals and owning animals have proved to be one of the best methods to engage the youth and ensure that they develop their skills faster.

If you have pet goats at home and are also parents to young children, you will see that your goats are your best tools to teach your little ones things like responsibility and ownership. Even if your children are very little, you can allow them to have supervised interactions with these goats for the best results.

You see, goats demand a great deal of attention. All the daily care activities for your goat need to be carried out twice a day. So, you can divide the responsibility between your children or among all the members of the family to make all of them responsible for the welfare of the animal.

With young children, the advantages are greater as they learn pretty soon that the goats are entirely dependent upon them. Once they have been assigned a responsibility and once they are in the groove, they will be attached enough to their pets to make sure that they are taken care of properly.

In addition to all this, goats teach children and young adults the very important quality of sensitivity. If you are actually breeding goats, you will find that your children are extremely sensitive as they are regularly interacting with new born kids. These delicate creatures require nurturing and care and your children will be able to provide them with just that.

Goats or any other pets can also provide a great source of learning about the concept of life and death. This is quite hard to teach young children. However, when it comes to coping with the death of a pet, when it happens it is known to make children stronger and more aware of the cycle of life.

Undoubtedly, their interaction with outdoor animals like the goat requires them to spend a great deal of time outdoors too. So, if you are worried about your child not getting enough exercise, you may consider buying him or her a goat.

4. Therapeutic

Goats are great companions. If you have been with them from their younger days, you will see that they actually grow quite fond of you. If you have just a pair of goats or a smaller herd, the attachment is greater as the attention you are able to give to each goat is quite high.

Goats can be extremely therapeutic to have at home. They love to go on long walks with their masters. It is possible to leash train your goat to go on walks with you. They will not complain either, as they will get enough food to eat along the way. While this is great to lift up your spirits, you will also find a good form of exercise that is investment free!

Goats also make very good hiking companions. If you make an effort to establish a good relationship with your goat, it can be really rewarding. Goats are known for being great backpacking partners. They love going on hikes and will also carry some of your belongings on their back. And, of course, they will have plenty to eat in the wilderness.

So, you see, there is more than one purpose of having a goat as a pet. Since they give so much love and are of such great use, it is your responsibility to ensure that your goats are taken care of properly.

Chapter 6: Where Do You Get Goats?

The most important thing that you need to do when you decide to bring home a pet goat is figure out where to get it from in the first place. However, even more important than that, know what kind of goat you want to bring home. At what stage of life should that pet be introduced into your home?

Before you get into the details of bringing a goat home, I would like to familiarize you with some common terminologies associated with goats. This will help you understand what exactly a breeder or a seller is trying to set you up with.

- **Buck:** A fully grown male goat is called a buck
- **Doe:** This is a fully grown, female goat
- **Buckling:** A baby buck
- **Doeling:** A baby doe
- **Wethers:** A male that has been neutered is called a wether.

When you go shopping for a pet, you can be quite overwhelmed. You can be sure of the breed that you want to buy when you are sure of why you are getting that breed in the first place. As we discussed before, there are several reasons why you may want a goat. There are some standard breeds that you can look for when you are planning to bring a goat home.

1. Traditional goat breeds

When you go to a breeder with the intention of bringing home a goat, you need to be aware of the breeds that are most popular or, rather, most traditional. Here is a list of some of the most popular goat breeds that goat lovers prefer to bring home:

Nubian Goats: These goats are considerably the most popular of all the goat breeds that we know of. They are large animals with distinct pendulous ears. They also have a roman nose. These goats originated in the United Kingdom and are descendants of the near east breeds. They are known for the high butterfat presence in their milk. As a result, they are highly preferred by individuals who are interested in the cheese making business.

Alpine Goats: As you can guess from the name of these goats, they originated in Switzerland. These goats were later taken to England and France where they gained popularity. Usually alpines are black and white in color. However, brown and white and other patterns have been observed, too. You can identify this breed by the curved and dished nose and the significantly upright ears. These are also primarily diary breeds.

Saanen and Sable: Saanens are usually off white or fully white in color. They are the largest among the dairy goats. A Saanen that is not white or off white is called a Sable. They usually depict a recessive gene that makes them appear different. These breeds are used in commercial dairies. They are friendly animals but they are difficult to maintain.

Oberhalsi: An oberhalsi is a variation of the Alpine Goat. They were recognised as a unique breed only recently. They are known for their erect ears and the distinct black marks on the back, legs, toes and belly. Sometimes these goats may also be pure black in color.

Toggenburg: Also known as the Toggs, these goats are available in a range of colors including fawn and chocolate brown that have distinct white markings. These goats resemble the Alpine goats. They are known for their long lactation periods. The milk of these goats is not as rich as other breeds but is low in butterfat content.

Pygmy Goat: The pygmy goat is a breed that was initially known as the Cameroon Dwarf Goat. This goat is usually found in the south western African countries. Sometimes they are also found in the eastern regions of Africa. This breed originated in the Cameron area in France. These goats were then displayed in Germany and Sweden as exotic animals. These goats are best as pets and are seldom used for any utility purposes.

The Boer Goat: This breed was developed in South Africa mainly for meat production. It is believed to be far superior to any other goat breed in quality of meat.

Cashmere Goats: The production of Cashmere goats is a relatively new industry in the United States. These goats were first brought to the USA from New Zealand and Australia in the late 1980s. They are bred for their fleece. An adult buck is capable of producing close to 2.5 pounds of fleece every year. This fleece consists of two types of hair: the Cashmere and the guard hair.

Angora: This breed is highly valued because of the mohair or the typical type of hair that is obtained from this goat. In the US an average goat can produce close to 5.3 pounds of mohair in each sheering! This mohair is very similar to the wool. However, it is softer, thinner and smoother.

The Myotonic Goat: as you know this goat is also called the fainting goat because of its characteristic 10 second muscle freeze when shocked or surprised. These goats are very special for goat owners because of their characteristic fainting abilities, of course but also for their amazing personalities. To honor these goats, there is a special Fainting Goat Festival that is held in Tennessee each year. The festival has several cultural displays and food stalls and is as large as any typical festival!

2. Age considerations for goats

Once you have decided on the breed that you want to bring home, the next thing you need to worry about is the age at which you want to bring the goat home. Now, usually, it is recommended that you bring home a baby, also known as a kid, buckling or doeling if you are a first time goat owner.

On the other hand, if you have had some experience with goats already and you feel ready to adopt an adult goat or even rescue an adult goat, you may do so. The care required and the source from which you can bring home these goats are quite different.

The younger the goat, the easier it is to train them. Babies also get more attached to you. They are calmer and more docile.

Therefore, they are easier to care for in comparison to adult goats.

Kids/ Doelings/ Bucklings

You can buy a kid that is one day old or even opt for one that is a couple of days old. There are several places where you can get your kids from. Most pet owners these days prefer to get their kids online. There are several reliable online barns or breeders' websites where you can get the goats of your choice.

> **Important note:** In my opinion, it is not very nice for a goat to be "shipped in a box". It is always better to collect the goat yourself from a breeder, even it if means you have to rent a vehicle to do so. I would personally never buy a goat that is shipped to me as I always go and collect my goats.
>
> However, I do realise that some people buy goats online and have them shipped therefore I am mentioning this in this book.

When you are looking at buying kids online, you need to do a good amount of research. Some of these online stores will have certain terms and conditions. The most common condition is that you need to buy a minimum number. Sometimes, they will need you to buy at least a pair of kids. Not all will have these conditions, but it is a good idea to check the terms.

Another common restriction is the weight. They may ship only a certain number of kids each time, provided that they are within a given weight limit, usually about 70 pounds. Goats are shipped to your home using services like the US postal service. They require special handling as well.

You can expect your pets to reach you in about three days' time. This information is given to you prior so that you can collect your goats. If you are not available to collect the goats, they will be left waiting in the post office without food or water. When you are ordering off the Internet, you also need to consider the weather conditions. If it is too hot or too cold, you will not be able to get them shipped from most breeders. Make sure you order them only when you have enough time on your hands to collect them on time.

When you go to collect your package, make sure you open and check if the goats are healthy. This is a policy that you need to pay great attention to. Most hatcheries will have all the terms and conditions regarding such an untoward incident mentioned on their website. You can also issue a claim at the post office if you feel like your kids have not been handled correctly.

With purchases that are made online, one needs to be extremely careful about where he is ordering from. Make sure you check all the reviews and testimonials correctly before you actually place the order. You can also get recommendations from friends and other goat owners. If you are certain that a particular website is completely reliable, you may go for it. If not, you must be open to other options to obtain your kids. You can be sure that a website is reliable if they have contact numbers that you can dial to speak with them. If they sound professional and are willing to answer all your queries and issues, you can rest assured. On the other hand, if they seem hesitant in providing you with details that you are looking for, you must think twice before making an investment.

The other option is to go in person and pick up the kids. There are several local farms and cooperatives where kids are sold. You can even buy them from your local pet store.

When you go in person, you can be a lot more confident of the quality of the kids that you are bringing home. If you notice any unhealthy goats in the place where you plan to buy the goats from, just turn around and walk home. If the housing areas have not been maintained well, it is an indication that the kids may be carrying deadly diseases. Even then, you must look for another option.

There are several preparations that you need to make before you bring the kids home. If they are being shipped to your home, you must understand that they have gone through a lot of stress. So, they will need a warm resting spot when they are back.

You must have plenty of water available for the goats to drink. Of course, you cannot place your water in deep bowls as the goats are too small. They may just tumble all the water and make a mess. You need to use small and shallow cups that they can drink from comfortably. The water must be changed on a regular basis to make sure that there is no infection or contamination. Most often, kids may be too frightened to drink water, but they really need it if they have been shipped. If you notice that one of your kids is not drinking the water that you have placed, you must lead it to the bowl so it can start drinking.

The next thing that you need to worry about is the feed. For babies, you may have to keep some milk and water ready. You can read about bottle feeding the kids in the following chapters. Make sure you have feeding bottles ready to welcome your goats. You must remember that kids are extremely delicate. So, you must not handle them too much. Even if you need to pick them up and check on them, you need to be extremely cautious. There are several reasons why you need to handle the goats. You may have to change the location or even clean the vent.

Kids are extremely cute and you may want to fondle them and really cuddle. However, remember that you must handle them only when it is absolutely necessary. Otherwise, you must leave them alone. Your baby pet will be stronger in a couple of days. That is when you can take them out and play with them.

3. Adult goats

If you are a first time owner, you need to be careful about bringing home an adult goat. This is the age when they are not as tender and delicate as the babies. However, they can be aggressive and might be a challenge to handle if you do not understand goat behaviour.

There are a couple of benefits of having adult goats. At that age, they do not need constant attention like the baby goats.. They are also structurally stronger which means that you need not worry about handling them too much or causing them any damage.

What you definitely need to check for is whether your adult goats have been neutered. If you have an intact adult male, you must be extremely cautious. They can get extremely aggressive and protective when the breeding season approaches. Adult goats are known to attack when they are threatened or even when they think that they are being threatened.

To help you out, I have discussed the typical behaviour patterns among adult goats in the next chapter. Once you know what to expect, you can be better prepared to handle the situation.

The age of the goat is a very important factor in deciding how the environment in your home will be. If you are purchasing a baby goat, the preparations are a lot more. On the other hand, an adult will only require a good enough house. The next set of questions that you need to ask yourself is the more practical one. When you are buying goats, only the age is not a deciding factor. There are several other things that determine where you will buy the goats from and how you plan to take care of them. Here are some questions you must ask yourself when you are planning to bring home goats, adults or babies.

4. Where to buy goats

When you have decided to bring home Fainting Goats, the next question is where to get them from? There are several options that are available to anyone who is interested in purchasing goats. Here are some options that you can try as far as goats are concerned.

Most importantly, you must check if you need a license to keep goats in the area you live in.

Online

To begin with, there are many websites where you will regularly find Fainting Goats on sale. These websites may belong to popular pet stores or even breeders. Sometimes, they might even be exclusive online stores that are meant to sell goats. There are several advantages of choosing your pet online. You do not have to make painful trips to barns and breeding farms that are located really far away from the city most of the times. Additionally, you will also be able to find great discounts when you buy your goats online.

Of course, the disadvantages are also present. You will have to rely on the seller's word as you will not be able to go and physically examine the animals when you make a purchase. This can be quite misleading. In addition to that, the shipping is always a risk to the health of little goats. Most often, they die if the travel distance is too long.

So, if you are really considering buying a goat online, make sure that you either shop from the websites of popular stores or that you look for recommendations from people who have made online purchases before. Unless you are completely sure of the authenticity and the reliability of a website, do not make any payments even if you feel like the costs are more than reasonable.

Goat Farms/ Barns

There are special goat farms or barns where breeders cultivate herds of various breeds. In these facilities, the babies are delivered and taken care of and then sold to interested buyers. This is a really booming industry especially for poultry and fish. The idea with these goat farms is to breed varieties that are rare or unusual for a specific region. With special breeds like the Fainting Goats, you will be able to find several farms that focus on this breed. There are two types of farms. There is one that produces baby goats through natural insemination and the other one that produces goats through artificial insemination. The latter usually focuses on the hybrids.

When you visit a barn to buy your goats, make sure that you check the health of the goat thoroughly before you make a purchase. Even if the goats that are sold to you look absolutely healthy, you must be sure that the goats are bred in healthy conditions. That is when you can be assured that the goats that you take home will remain healthy.

Ask for a health certificate for the livestock that is sold to you. In most barns and farms, the kids are vaccinated within a few days of birth. You must also check for this before you buy the goats so that you know if you will have to take them to the vet before you take them home.

Livestock Organisations

There are several national and local livestock organisations where you can pick up your goats. These organisations usually focus on producing goats that are of show quality. There are also several Fainting Goat Clubs and Associations that you will be able to locate in your zip code. The advantage of buying in these clubs is that you will have beautiful goats that are maintained as per all the standards recommended normally.

Of course, the goats that you buy from such places might seem really expensive. However, for those of you who have business interests in keeping the herd, it is an investment that is completely worth it. You can check on the club website for details on the recommended standards so that you do not end up paying too much for a goat that is nowhere near show standards.

Breeders

With popular breeds like the Fainting Goats, there will be several individual breeders who will be able to get you healthy specimens for your home. The advantages of getting a goat from a good breeder are many, especially if you are a first time owner. When you have a reliable breeder to help you out, he will become the best consultant next to your veterinarian with respect to proper care for your goats. Breeders will also be able to help you convert your hobby into a lucrative business as they will be able to provide you with leads for your sales.

When you buy from an individual breeder, make sure that you visit his set up once before you buy your beloved pet. The most important thing is the condition in which your breeder is raising the goats. If you see that the shelters have not been cleaned for a long time, you must be very careful. Especially, faeces deposited around the shelters means that the animals could be harboring dangerous diseases. If you already have a herd of your own, you will be jeopardising the health of the entire herd if you neglect this important part.

Your breeder must also be able to provide you with a health certificate for the goats that you buy. If the breeder is hesitant to provide you with one, it is recommended that you look for another one who is okay with giving you a certificate.

Whenever you go to a local breeder, look for recommendations. If you are new to raising, speak to friends or relatives who have already had goats at home. They should be able to help you out. You may even want to take someone reliable with you when you go to a breeder for the first time. That way even the breeder will be aware that you know what you are talking about and that he cannot get away with giving you unhealthy goats for your home.

Rescue Shelters

Another interesting option is adopting goats for your backyard. This is considered an extremely humane option as there are several goats who really require care and help. The best part about this is also that you can bring home the animals for free!

If you have decided to adopt kids or even an adult buck or doe, here are a few steps that you need to take in order to actually bring home the pet of your choice.

The first thing that you need to do is contact your local authorities about adoption in your state. There are some rules that you will need to abide by depending upon the part of the world that you are residing in. In some zones, adoption is not as easy as picking a goat and bringing it home. You need to get a few permits and licenses for your backyard goats. If you are looking at a business with the goats that you are adopting, there may be several more rules that are applicable to you.

The next thing is to look for an organisation that is putting up livestock for adoption. You can ask for assistance at veterinary hospitals or even your local municipality. There are several rescue shelters in each area. If you are still unable to find a good place, just look online. The other advice I have is for you to look in the agricultural or rural areas. You are most likely to find great options in these areas.

When you have chosen an organisation that you want to adopt from, you can send in a request. The best thing to do would be to actually visit the place to adopt your goats. You must be prepared for a full-fledged interview when you are out to adopt a Fainting Goat. The thing is most of these shelters want to ensure that the animals that they rescue do not go back to living in cruel conditions. They will, therefore, ask you about the space that you have to accommodate the goats, details about your other pets, your source of funds to support the animals that you are adopting etc. So, if you are going to adopt a goat, there are things that you want to consider before you meet the authorities.

If you show the slightest signs of hesitation or lack of knowledge, your chances of bringing home those beautiful goats are greatly reduced. Now, you definitely do not want that to happen, do you?

Once you have convincingly answered all the questions, you will be allowed to take a look at the goats that are up for adoption. When you have found the ones that you think you want to take home, you can fix a date and time when you want to pick them up. When you have finalised on the goats, make sure you ask about the fees, if any. Sometimes, there is a small municipality fee that you will have to pay before you adopt. However, in most cases, adoption is free.

It is a good thing to adopt multiple goats at one time. That way, you will be able to give your beloved goats some friends to hang around with while you are out or away at work.

No matter what option you choose with respect to bringing home a goat, you must be fully aware that the responsibility that you will have is very high. You must be prepared to transform parts of your home into suitable environments for these animals that you will be sharing your home with.

If you already have a herd or other pets at home, the challenges that you will face are different. While you would have decent experience with respect to the care that the goats need, you will have to worry about things like ensuring that the animals in your home are able to live together comfortably.

For first time owners, everything can be a challenge that you have to overcome. While this journey is actually a lot of fun, it can be overwhelming if you do not have the right assistance.

This book is designed to help you overcome these challenges. Of course, the first thing that you will need help with is understanding how much you can handle. There are several considerations before you actually welcome a pet goat into your home. There are some very important questions that you need to ask yourself before you go out there to buy or adopt goats. The next part of this chapter will help you find the answers to these questions as well. Only when you are convinced about your choice of having goats as pets should you take up this big responsibility.

Chapter 7: Making A Home For Your Goats

A goat is quite different from a regular pet that you would bring home. For instance, it is more common for people to have a dog or a cat in their home. However, a goat might seem unusual. If you are not completely prepared for it, you may experience a lot of issues when you bring home a pet goat. So there are some things that you need to do in advance before you make your home a safe haven for goats.

1. Preparing the family

Your entire family needs to be aware of the responsibility that comes with having pet goats at home. Since these pets are not your ordinary fuzzy and furry pets, you need to understand that your family also needs some getting used to. If you simply love the idea of having a goat at home, here are some tips that will help you make your family enjoy the whole process as well:

• First talk to your family about your pet choice. If you have an enthusiastic family, this may not be much trouble. However, if you feel like your family is sceptical about the whole idea, you may want to give them some information on why having a pet goat can actually be advantageous.

• Check your family for allergies. You must be sure that your family does not have any member who is allergic to farm animals. If you have been frequently visiting farms and agricultural areas, you might already be familiar with the allergies present in your family. On the other hand, if you think that not everyone has had as much experience with farm animals as yourself, you might want them to get tested by experts.

• If you have a family member who does not approve of this idea, reconsider the option of bringing home a goats.

• If you are certain that you will be bringing home a pet goat, choose the breed that you want to bring home along with your entire family. It is quite fun to go out to various barns and farms to check out the breeds that are available. This is especially important if you have kids in your home. They must be part of the entire decision making process so that they feel a sense of responsibility towards the pet.

• Involve your family in the knowledge gaining process. Watch informative videos, make small notes or even read books together. The more everyone knows about livestock care, the better it is for you and your new pet. Gather as much information as you can about the proper caring methods for goats.

• Make sure that they are all present when you bring home the goats for the first time. This will make them involved in the process of raising the goats right from the beginning.

• Assign responsibilities to each member of the family. Again, this is particularly important if you have children at home. They need to understand the fact that having goats at home is not just fun and games. Give them simple tasks like feeding the goats. Children must never be given the job of cleaning as they may catch serious infections and diseases.

• Make sure that everyone in your family is aware of how to handle the goats properly. Especially if you are bringing home small baby goats, they need to be taken care of rather delicately. If your family keeps on touching them and fondling them, they will get anxious and, in worst cases, injured.

• If there are children at home, tell them that the new pet is not a toy. Your child must never tease or trouble the animal. While something as simple as a pat on the head is permissible, make sure that kids do not kiss or hug the animal too close. There are serious infections that may be transmitted to children. Also, if the goat is slightly older, it may harm the child in the process of defending itself. Never let the child pull the ears or even squeeze the goats to hard. While they may seem cute and cuddly, larger goats can be nasty when they are defensive.

2. The initial days

The first few days can be really hard for your Fainting Goats and you. When they have just arrived in your home, it is natural for you to feel all excited and a little nervous, of course. You may spend the first few days obsessing about the behavior of your goats. You can never be certain if they are behaving in the right way or not because you are not sure if you have provided them with the perfect ambience to thrive well in. So in the first few days, here are some tips that will really help you:

• Leave them alone for a while. If you are keeping them indoors, especially, the last thing that you want to worry about is predators. Allow your goats to explore the area that they are going to live in for the next few years of their lives. If you are constantly checking on them, they may not be able to do this comfortably.

• The next thing that you need to do is make sure that they have a warm and comfortable space to be in. We will get into the details in the next part of this chapter.

• Goats can be overwhelmed easily. So if you have a pet at home, keep it away from your goat for the first few days. Also avoid loud noises and sounds around the new members of your family. You definitely do not want to have the goat associating you with dreadful noises.

• If they are not eating properly or are very quiet, leave them alone. They are probably tired from the journey if they have been shipped. In case you have shifted them to a new shelter as well, they will be too scared to even eat properly.

• Keep an eye on your goats. Always observe their behaviour.

3. Introducing a goat to an existing herd

The hardest part about bringing home goats is introducing them to a herd that is already in your home. The reason this is so hard is that when you try to mix different breeds of goats in one flock there are chances of fights and squabbles. You need to be extremely careful to ensure the safety of the new animals and also the safety of the goats in your current flock. If you have two males, especially, the issues are a lot more than you can imagine.

Goats are rather social animals. So, understanding their behaviour is not exactly the hardest thing to do. However, you must remember that like every herd animal, even the goats depict a certain pecking order. When you are introducing new goats to your flock, there are several things that could go wrong unless you get the introduction right.

In order to get the introduction right, you need to understand a natural process known as "the pecking order". In fact, the pecking order is so important in goats that they will actually fight nastily to get positions that they are trying for.

Herd behaviour in goats

Goats look like really pleasant creatures. So, it is natural for most owners to think that when you bring home a goat and introduce it to the existing herd, they will simply get along with each other and miraculously become one happy family.

Well, most goat owners wish that the process was that simple. Especially with smaller breeds like the Fainting Goat, this is a matter of great concern. So before you just give your existing herd new "friends", you may want to take a couple of important precautions.

When there is a herd that is already existing in your home, you need to understand that there is a pecking order that have already been established. Each doe or buck in that group has its own personality. Hence, the order in which they dominate the group has already been established.

There is a rather practical reason for establishing the pecking order in a herd. This is the best way to curb aggression in a herd. It is also true that the pecking order may change from one day to another depending upon the behaviour of the goats.

There are three factors that determine the dominance of a member in a herd. The gender, the age and the presence or absence of horns. Every doe remains dominant over the female kids that she has delivered for years on end. If you have bucks in your group, you will see that they are always more dominant over the females.

Goats engage in a bizarre head butting ritual to establish their spot in the herd. The goat that remains adamant till the end of the ritual becomes the leader of the group. So, if you have goats with no horns, they will be defeated faster.

The buck that leads the herd or is the most dominant of the rest is called the Top Buck. His responsibilities include taking care of the herd and protecting it. If you notice herd movements, you will always see the Top Buck at the end of the herd. If the Top Buck dies or is removed, the rituals are repeated to choose the next leader.

There is also a dominant doe that is always present in a herd. This doe is known as the "Flock Queen". The job of the queen is to lead the entire herd and take them to the best spots for grazing. Herds find it a little harder to determine the Flock Queen. You will observe a sense of confusion when the Flock Queen is removed from the herd.

Here is an interesting ritual that I have heard about and even seen in a herd. If a Flock Queen notices a poisonous plant, she will sniff it and show signs of disgust. Then, the entire herd will sniff that plant and memorize it. In the end, the Top Buck just tramples that plant. So, if you see any trampled plants in your yard, you know why this is happening.

However, always make it a point to observe your herd well. If you notice serious injuries or very aggressive fights, you may consider taking the new goats out of the herd for a while. There are many issues that you must consider when you introduce a new goat to the herd. I have provided a list below. Make sure you give each one serious thought to ensure the best health for your flock.

• Quarantining: Although most new goats look healthy from the outside, there are chances that they will destroy your entire herd if you are not careful enough. So, when you are introducing a new goat into your herd, make sure that you take all the quarantining measures necessary. It is recommended that you quarantine the new goats for at least 30 days. The best thing to do would be to keep the new goats in a separate space for two weeks. Observe them to make sure that they do not ruin the well-being of the existing herd.

• Size matters: If you are adding a Fainting Goat to a group of large goats, it might be an issue. Similarly, if you add a younger goat, you may see that he will get bullied by the older members of a herd. So, when you are adding a new goat to the herd, make sure that he is a fully mature goat that is of a decent size.

• Distract the existing herd: If the goats in your existing herd have something new to catch their attention, they may not trouble the new member as much. You could add a toy like a climbing table or even a few spring greens to spare your newcomers the tension.

• Keep them divided: It is a good idea to use a make shift fence when you are introducing a new goat to the herd. This will give them a safe space in which they can get accustomed to the existing herd. Even the existing herd will become used to the sights and sounds of the newcomers.

• Make sure there is enough food: If the food containers are plenty, there will be fewer reasons to squabble and fight. Also, the new goats are often scared. So, they need to have enough food that they know that they can eat safely. If you cannot ensure this, they will probably just stick to their part of the shelter and never get out.

• Make enough room: If your goats have enough space, they will not get in each other's face. You must always let the herd out in the open for a while. This will help the goats that are getting hassled run away to a safer spot, thus avoiding serious injuries.

• Keeping bucks together: We have all heard of bucks fighting quite aggressively. So if you are introducing a buck to a flock that already has bucks in it, you might have to take a lot of precautions. The best thing to do is to place the younger bucks with the older ones in an enclosure for a while, separating them with a temporary fence. The older goats actually teach the youngsters how to behave!

• Introductions at night: if you plan to introduce the new goats to the herd at night or when it is dark, make sure that you are there almost at the break of dawn. If the current herd wakes up to a new member suddenly, they may become so overwhelmed that they may head butt or trample him to death.

• Keep the age groups different: This is a pretty important tip. To begin with, the older goats tend to be a lot more dominating. Additionally, there may also be some infections within a group that the younger goats are not immune to.

The best introductions

If you plan to introduce new goats to the group, the best way to do it would be to actually place the newer goats in a fenced area in the space that your current herd is already using. This approach is best preferred as the new goats have a space that they can be safe in. At the same time, they will face the existing goats regularly. When this type of interaction occurs, both the groups feel less threatened in each other's presence. Eventually, they will get accustomed to the sights and sounds of each other and will be less aggressive when they are placed in the same house together.

Another approach that is rather interesting is placing both groups in a new house and a new space. Since the space is new to both the groups, the pecking order has still not been established. The process of establishing the order will not change much. However, the level of aggression will be much lesser when the goats are introduced in a completely new environment. All you need to do is ensure that they have ample space for themselves. You must also provide your goats with enough food so that they do not have too many reasons to be aggressive.

Sometimes, there might be one particular goat that is extremely aggressive. If you are able to identify this goat, you must take it away from the group. It is alright even if this goat belongs to your existing herd. That way, it will become easier for the pecking order to be established in the group. When you know that your current group of goats are living together in peace, reintroduce the aggressive goat. Now, he is the newcomer and will be toned down by the established pecking order.

Sometimes, it may seem like a lot of effort when you try to introduce a new bunch of goats to an existing flock. However, you do not have too many options when you are in a goat business. You must always rotate your herd. While this may seem challenging in the beginning. It will be a walk in the park as you progress and get used to the process.

4. Introducing your goats to pets

Another matter of great concern is introducing your Fainting Goats to the pets that you have at home. There are two possibilities when you bring home a goat. Your existing pets will become great friends with it, or, they will be foes! Either way, you need to introduce the goats to your family pets.

Think of introducing pets to goats as introducing a new baby brother or sister to a child. Of course, there will be an initial phase of tantrum throwing and jealousy. However, as time goes on, things will be alright. All you need to do is supervise the toddler and the infant during this period of acclimatization.

If you have a pet that you keep indoors, you may argue that it is not necessary to have the introduction as they may never meet. However, don't forget that even the cat or dog that you have in your home loves to go out once in a while. The garden and the yard in your home is a space that your family pets love too. If you ignore the introduction, you may have to witness sudden and rather unpleasant ones!

The introduction should never be hurried. Make sure that the animals have enough space and time to get used to each other. You must also be very careful to ensure that both the animals are completely protected.

When you are introducing your pet and the goat for the first time, try to keep the goat in an enclosure. You must also tie your family pet up during the introduction. The last option is to hold the goat in your arms during the introduction. Whatever you do, make sure that the introduction is fully supervised. Since you are not sure about the reaction, you must never take any chances.

If you have a pet cat at home, the most important thing to understand is that the garden is as much the cat's territory as it is the goat's territory. Cats are naturally very curious and they tend to poke around in the garden. They are usually more interested in the rodents than the goats. So the introduction of cats and goats are a lot safer.

On the other hand, if you are trying to introduce your goat to a dog, the precautions that you need to take are greater. It is always best that you introduce your pet dog to goats when he is still a puppy. You see, there are some breeds of dogs that can be used to herd the goats, too if they are trained well. However, if your dog is not sure about interacting with goats, he may attack. Remember, that goats can also be aggressive, making the interaction fatal for either animal in worst cases.

It is true that dogs are considered as suitable guardians to goats. There are several families who will leave the dog alone with the goats. This is alright when the goats and dogs are in a garden setting where the goats have enough space to escape if the dog becomes aggressive. However, there are also many tragic instances when several members of a herd have been destroyed because the dog's instincts kick in.

It is definitely recommended that you be extremely protective with your goats. At the same time, be patient with your canine friend. Always make sure that the introductions are in a protected environment. The goats should be in an enclosed space till you know that the dog is used to their presence. The next step would be to directly introduce the two while the goat is in your arms.

If your dog has been trained well, it is a bonus. If he can "heel" and "stay" at your command, your goats are safer. You may also keep your dog on a leash when the goats are free range. Once the goats are not "new" or interesting to your dog, you can be more assured that he will be easily distracted by other things. Most often, dogs will find squirrels more interesting that the goats that they see on a daily basis. So, if you want your pets to be at peace with each other, make sure that they spend plenty of time with each other.

Also, you must be open to the fact that some breeds are more aggressive than the others. So, even when you are introducing family pets over and over to the goats, you cannot be sure that the goats are entirely safe. Of course, they will get used to each other. However, whether they can really be the best of friends is an entirely different question.

The most tragic thing is knowing that your dog or cat can be harmful for your herd. In most cases, you will know that your dog or cat is harmful only after a serious injury or in worst cases, a fatality. In such cases, you will have to choose between your goat and your existing pet. Of course, in most cases the pet that has been with an owner for longer gets preference. There is no reason to be upset with your family pet as the reaction is just the result of a very strong instinct.

5. The final checklist

When you are bringing home a new pet, there are so many things that you need to worry about that you might simply forget a few in all the excitement. This checklist is for all you beginners who are already fumbling with the right preparations to make your home a perfect place to raise healthy goats in.

- Get permission from your local authorities
- Inform your neighbors
- Make enough space for the animals
- Prepare the shelters
- Get comfortable and warm bedding
- Prepare sleeping shelves
- Prepare feeders
- Place many waterers
- Keep manure boxes handy
- Keep the feed ready
- Make sure you have access to kidding needs
- Keep probe thermometers handy
- Storage containers
- Keep heaters for younger goats
- Buckets for milking

We will discuss in greater detail about these supplies in the following chapters. When you are preparing your home for a goat or a herd, make sure that you have everything that you need handy. This will make the transition and acclimatization easier for the animal. You will also feel less overwhelmed if you have everything in place to welcome your new members. You will find all the supplies you need at local pet stores or even online.

Chapter 8: Housing Your Fainting Goats

The type of housing that you make for your goats determines how safe and healthy they will be. One of the most important things to do when you bring home goats is building a good shelter for them.

In addition to a good resting place, you also need to make sure that you get good fencing around your property to keep the goats safe. Like I mentioned in the previous chapters, goats require a rather sturdy fencing to keep them safe inside the property.

There are several dangers out there that can seriously jeopardize the well-being of your herd. So, you must make sure that they have a safe environment to live in peacefully. So when you bring home goats, you need to build proper housing facilities because:

- Predators are always on the prowl. Goats make very easy targets. You need to also remember that goat meat is extremely delicious and there are several predators out there that are looking for a good meal.

- Goats are also capable of running away. If the space that they are kept in is not enclosed, they might wander away and be seriously injured.

- Free range pets are most often killed by traffic. If your farm or home is close to a busy freeway, you must be additionally cautious when you bring home a goat.

- Goats require a warm shelter at night to remain healthy. They may feel uncomfortable and even threatened if that does not happen.

1. Building the perfect shelter for your goats

Your goat needs a good shelter to stay in at nights. When they feel threatened or uncomfortable, goats will usually take shelter in the housing area. You must also make sure that the goats have a good enough space to stay in when the weather is bad. You must be extra careful when you build the housing area if you intend to breed goats. When the babies are delivered, both the baby and the mother require a good resting area.

Here are some considerations that you must bear in mind when you are building your goat a shelter.

- Space is the most important consideration when it comes to the housing of your goats. You must measure the height and the weight of the shelter accurately when you are building the shelter. On average, a goat will require close to 10 to 15 square feet of resting area. They also need to have space outside the shelter.

You must also consider your comfort when it comes to building your goat a home. You need to be able to muck the bedding or clean it easily. If the goat shelter is shorter than you, make sure that it isn't too deep or else you will have a hard time cleaning.

- The flooring of the shelter needs to be given some thought. You need to find a flooring option that is easy to maintain as well as one that is comfortable for the goats to reside in. Usually, goat owners prefer to have dirt or gravel flooring for the shelters. Some may even opt for wood. However, I would recommend dirt flooring as it can absorb urine well. In addition to that, the floor can be really warm when you just cover it with some straw. A concrete flooring is an absolute no because it is hard and really cold. Many pet owners choose this because it is easier to clean. However, I would never recommend it.

- If the shelter is not well ventilated, the herd won't thrive well. At the same time, there should not be any drafts as the animals will not be able to keep themselves warm at night. The best way to ensure that you get the best of both worlds is to keep the airflow high while allowing the goats to rest below. You must remember that having livestock will increase the levels of moisture within the shelter. The ammonia contained in their faeces is also high. So if these elements are not vented out regularly, the repercussions can be serious.

- The temperature within the shelter is very important. It is alright to have an open resting space with good fencing if the weather is warm enough. However, on the other hand, if you live in an area that is exceptionally cold, you may want to reconsider the housing area. The drainage of the coop must be good enough to make sure that it stays warm even when it is raining or snowing heavily outside.

- The size of your herd is of great importance. If you plan to increase the size of your herd over time, you need to make sure that you start off with a large enough space in the beginning. If not, you must be prepared to build more shelters over time. You must also have separate housing areas for the does, bucks and the kids that need to be weaned from the mother.

- You also need to have a decent storage space near the shelter that you can access easily. This space should be accessible to you but out of your herd's reach.

- Another concern with shelters is burrowing animals. If there are rats or mice, you must also protect the shelter from them to ensure that the food supplies are safe. For this, you can lay fencing wire around the coop. Bury it in the ground up to about 15 cms. If pests try to get into the shelter by making a burrow, they will be blocked by the metal wires.

- Irrespective of the breed that you have, you need to make sure that you have a designated are for routine care such as trimming the hair and clipping. If you are raising goats for milk, this additional space can also double as a milking space for your goat.

- You must also plan for kidding pens that are 4 feet by 5 feet in dimension if you plan to raise kids on your property.

- Once the shelter has been made completely, make sure you check it again. Any protruding wire or nail in the coop can cause serious injuries to the herd.

You see, building a safe shelter is not rocket science. All you need to do is ensure that the animals are warm and safe while they have ample space to move around. In keeping this as the basic need for a shelter, you can choose to easily build one on your own. Livestock shelters have been developed over the years to make them easily adaptable in the urban set up.

When you are building a shelter for your goat, you must consider all the space and economic restrictions that you may face. When you have a budget in mind, you will be able to build a suitable shelter. You must also be aware of the ways in which you will utilise your shelter. Here are a few tips to build a good shelter when you are on a tight budget.

2. Budget shelter options

The utility and the budget of a shelter determine the size and the type of housing. You can make something really simple or can build a really spectacular structure for your goat. However, it is good to keep the investment to the required amount so that you have enough funds if you want to build more shelters in the future or expand the one that you already have. Here are a few budget options for your goats' shelter.

Building using wooden pellets

The best thing to do when you are taking up the project of building your goat's shelter is to recycle the stuff that you have lying around your farm. If you have wooden pallets available, you can build a sturdy three sided housing for your goats. You will need some plywood to cover it up thoroughly.

In case you don't have wood pallets in your home, there are several places where you can get them from. You can even get it for free or for a very small fee. These pallets are available at industries, building sites, larger farms and dedicated farm supply stores.

The ideal size of each pallet should be about 2 by 4. You will need plywood to cover it. You also need some sturdy roofing material. Many goat owners that I know prefer to use spare metal sheets that are also available from the places mentioned above.

These shelters can protect the goats from rain and sun. Typically, a shelter like this can house about four medium sized goats.

Quonset hut or a cattle panel

A shelter like this is usually used for goats that are meat yielding. These shelters can provide protection in the milder climatic zones. It is usually open on both the ends and just acts as a roof or shade for the goat. These cattle panels are considered strong enough to hold out snow in some cases. This is true when the tarp quality is excellent and when they have been nailed to the ground really well. It is always recommended that you build such a shelter next to a barn. So, in worst cases, the goats can seek shelter quickly if the tarp hut or panel is unable to withstand severe weather conditions.

A Dog Run

Dog runs can make great houses for smaller goats. All you need is a cover that is made of a water resistant fabric like tarpaulin. When the weather gets too cold, all you need to do is cover the run fully or partly with the tarp. If you also have a good dog house, you can make great sleeping quarters by putting the run inside the dog house. The idea is to ensure that the run is covered properly at night. This allows you to provide security to the herd even at night. You can be assured that predators will not get into the run.

A Wood Frame Shelter

This is easily the best option for housing goats as it is a very flexible option. You can build a wood frame shelter of any size you like. You also have the freedom of choosing the material that you want to work with when you build the house. You can combine the wooden frame with metal and create a sturdy roof. You can also use shingle as a roofing option.

These shelters may have a door, which makes them more secure. If you are sure of the type of fencing that you have, you can even have a partly enclosed one or one with an opening on one side.

All you need to ensure with any type of housing is good draining. The goats must feel warm and secure in these homes.

3. Creating the perfect ambience

It is not enough to simply build a shelter for your goats. You need to make sure that the space is utilised fully. This is possible only when the ambience within the shelter is perfect for your herd to thrive in.

When you build a shelter, you must equip it with everything that your goats will require. Whether they are resting after delivering kids or whether they are carrying out mundane daily activities, your shelter must facilitate it completely. There are a few installations that you must make inside or around the shelter in order to create the perfect ambience for your goats. The three most essential things along with the shelter are:

A sleeping shelf

Goats may sleep indoors or they may just rest outside. This depends entirely upon the weather conditions. However, it is a good idea to have sleeping shelf for your goats to rest. You can build this sleeping shelf in the housing area or in some other building on the farm (a barn or shed). The most recommended type of sleeping shelf is the triangular one in the corner. These shelves are extremely cosy and are not very space consuming.

You can build a simple sleeping shelf using plywood. It is best that you use pressure treated plywood to ensure that the goats remain on a sturdy surface all night long.

There is another advantage of having sleeping shelves, besides making a good resting space, which is that the kids will have a safe space where they will not get trampled or hurt. If these kids are not sleeping with their moms, they can also sleep under the shelves to stay protected always.

Waterer

You must ensure that goats are never kept without water. Many goat owners have a misconception that goats may drink too much water and actually die. Hence they keep the waterers away from the goats while feeding them.

This practice is never recommended as goats require water more than food. Especially when you are feeding the goats dry pellets, you must make sure that you provide water alongside. When goats eat dry pellets or crumbs and fail to have an adequate amount of water, the feed begins to swell inside the animal. The risk of choking is also high when goats are given dry food without water.

So, make sure that you always have enough clean drinking water for the goats.

Feeders

The biggest challenge with goats is to monitor their feed and to make sure that they eat regularly. If you are not able to do this hands on, you can use a food dispenser that works quite well.

The most basic type of food dispenser consists of a plastic dome like structure that has a roof to keep the food dry. It has a small feeder around it where the goats can eat. The beauty of this dispenser is that it keeps refilling the feeder as the goats finish eating. So, all you need to do is fill the dispenser regularly and be care free.

Another interesting type of food dispenser is the tread plate feeder. With this type of feeder, a metal tread plate provides access to the food. Every time a goat steps on this feeder, it will open the lid to the container which stores the feed.

An automatic pet feeder is only useful when you have smaller herds. These feeders are ideal to feed one or two pets each time. So if you have between 2 to 4 goats, this type of feeder might work well for you.

Automatic pet feeders have been designed for people who are unable to stay at home all day to ensure that their pets are being fed on time. It is possible to program close to 10 meals each day for your goat. You can set the program to dispense an exact amount of feed each time. You also have the option of setting different portions each time.

You can time these automatic feeders and be assured that your pet goats will not remain hungry. Like I mentioned before, goats are not really dependent on their owners for their food. They can easily forage around for their food. In case you have to keep your goat indoors for some reason, this type of feeder works best. For instance, if your goat has undergone any surgery or is under treatment, he may not be able to forage. In such cases an automatic dispenser works best.

Besides making your life easier, food dispensers serve several other purposes. Now, goats poop so often. Undoubtedly, they also remain hungry all the time and constantly require food. With a food dispenser you can ensure that your precious pets have access to food all the time.

A common problem that most goat owners face is finding poop in the food very often. Using a food dispenser puts an end to this rather difficult problem. Also, you will not have to deal with upturned bowls of food. This reduces wastage and ensures that the food is stored in hygienic conditions.

4. Bedding options for Goats

The bedding that you place in the coops should be made from a material that will be able to keep the goats warm and dry throughout. It must also be easy to clean. If the material that you are using has the property of retaining water, then you will notice that it will be very hard to maintain the shelter well. So, for best results, you must use the following bedding options in your shelter:

Pine Shavings: This is the most preferred type of bedding option as goats simply love it. It is ideal for smaller herds. The best thing about pine shavings is that they are highly absorbent. They have the ability to soak in not only the wetness but also the odor of the poop. They help you manage the litter well. Additionally, pine shavings are also very soft and light. The shavings are extremely easy to replace. They are also highly affordable and easily available. If you are buying pine shavings online, make sure you don't get confused between chips and shavings. Pine chips are terrible bedding options.

Straw and Hay: This is a popular bedding choice among people who have small farms. The reason that it is so popular is that it is extremely affordable and really durable. It is also a good absorbent that has the ability to soak the wetness and also soak the odor. The quality of the straw and hay is important. If you compromise on this, the straw will remain moist, making the shelter smell really bad.

Shredded Paper: In case you run out of your regular bedding material, shredded paper can make a great alternative. It is also considered one of the most popular trends among livestock owners. This is not only a good bedding option but is also a great way to recycle paper. The best thing is that you will never run out of it. All you need to do is shred the newspaper in your home into small pieces and lay it on the floor neatly. Newspaper shredding is a great absorbent like any other bedding material. The goats will not be harmed by it at all.

Dirt: Dirt is a really interesting option for shelter bedding. The first and the most important thing is that dirt is completely natural. Hence, it will not harm the animals even a little. Sand along with animal poop can make great compost.

Sawdust: This is a rather novel idea in the world of livestock keeping. Sawdust is great as it is really soft. Sawdust also has a natural smell that keeps the coop fresh all day long. During the colder months, sawdust makes a great bedding option as it can be really warm. The only disadvantage with saw dust is that it retains water. It is also prone to bacteria. So, you must make sure that you change the sawdust regularly if you choose to use it.

When you are choosing the bedding option for the shelter, there is one more thing that you must consider. If your goats are sharing the space with another pet, you must avoid bedding that will not suit the other animal.

5. Keeping predators at bay

The biggest problem with having goats in your garden is the danger of predators. It is heart-breaking when you realize that one of your beauties has been taken away or killed by a predatory animal. Of course, this is a natural process that you cannot really stop. What you can do is keep your goats in enclosures when you are not around to supervise, especially at night. You can also build fences to keep the predators away from your herd.

The difficult part is that goats are usually extremely vulnerable when they are domesticated. So, they become easy prey for animals like coyotes and foxes or even bobcats and raccoons. With animals like the coyote, you can even expect attacks in broad daylight. So you must take several preventive measures to ensure that your goats are safe. Some methods you can use are:

- Allow your goats out in the open. This is required for them to survive. However, if you have noticed attacks during the day, make sure you have someone to supervise the herd.

- Get rid of possible hiding spots for predators. Coyotes, especially, love hiding in thick bushes before attacking the goats.

- Getting a dog will help if your predator problem comes from bobcats. They are effective against other animals, too. However, bob cats can be kept at bay only with dogs as no fence or enclosure will stop them.

- Direct your goats into enclosures every night. You can even use temporary fencing if you notice that the animals are sleeping outdoors.

- Use fences as the primary defence against predators.

- Do not leave garbage out in the open. Usually, predators like raccoons are first attracted by the smell of the garbage. If you can keep your space clean, you can avoid such animals.

If you think that predators are a serious problem, you may also contact your Environment Protection Council. They will be able to give you more definite methods to keep predators away. If the problem still persists, keeping the goats in spacious enclosures is the best option. You can create the right environment for the goats within this environment so that they continue to forage and have a good time.

The best way to control predators is to use fencing around your home. There are several fencing options that can be used. Some of them can also be used to direct and control your herds.

6. Fencing options

Temporary fencing

Temporary fencing serves two purposes. It can be used to separate various farm animals and can also be used to direct them into their enclosures. The primary function of a temporary or portable fence is to mark boundaries and actually control your animal groups.

The most common type of temporary fence is the chain link fence. You can get long rolls of chain links that are arranged in a zigzag pattern. The heavy base allows you to place them where you need. Another simple type of temporary fencing is the mesh fence. It is similar to the chain link fence but is more secure as the base is heavier.

For larger animals like the goat, you can also use a picket fence. They have vertically arranged wires that have a very strong base to keep these animals safe.

If you have poultry in your home, you can use chicken wires or poultry fences to keep goats and chickens separate. These fences are ready to install and can be adjusted as per your needs. They do not require any tools for installation and work perfectly well on all terrains.

Permanent fencing

Permanent fences do not serve the purpose of separating different farm animals. They are used to mark the boundary of your garden to prevent animals from getting out or getting in to your property. For instance, if you have a freeway near your home, a permanent fence will keep your goats from getting away from your garden or farm. They also keep predators at bay.

Needless to say, these structures, once installed must not be removed. They must also be able to keep small animals and birds from getting in and out. In addition to that, they must also be strong enough to hold on for several years.

The most common type of permanent fencing used to keep your goats safe is the wooden or bamboo fencing. Panels of wood and bamboo are installed around the perimeter of your space. You must make sure that there are no gaps in between panels. Concrete fences are also used. They are sturdier and are also great at keeping predators away.

Electric fences are not my favourite option. Of course, many blogs and websites suggest them as an effective way to keep predators away. However, there are chances that your own pets will get electrocuted. Of course, it is a cruel option whether you are thinking of keeping predators or pets in their boundaries.

Chapter 9: Goat Care Essentials

When you bring home goats, you need to understand that all their daily care routines are twice a day jobs. This means that you have to feed them twice, clean up twice and even change their water twice a day. That means, the responsibility of owning a goat is double the responsibility of owning any other pet.

The first thing that you need to worry about is feeding your goats properly. They need to get the right nutrition if you want them to stay active and fit. The feeding demands of baby goats are quite different from the adult goats and you need to prepare as per the age of the members of your flock.

1. Feeding goats

Feeding baby goats

Normally baby goats are fed by the mother till a certain age and then they are fed with adult goat food. However, when the goats are used for the milk business the baby goats are not allowed to feed on the mother. In such cases and also when the goat is an orphan the baby goats are fed with bottled milk.

There is a step by step programme that has been devised to bottle feed the baby goat. The first thing you need to do is put together the basic things required to execute the programme.

The things required are:

- A Milk Source: It could either be whole cow milk or whole raw goat milk. If you are using raw milk make sure that it is from a herd which is CAE CL etc. free, otherwise you need to pasteurise the milk.

- A bottle (could either be pop bottle or water bottle)

- A nipple (you may use lambar nipples on pop bottle till they are able to drink out of lambar feeder)

- A pot

- A measuring cup

- A hungry baby

Measure the amount of milk required. Baby goats are normally given one quart per day per kid. If you are feeding the babies twice a day then you will need 2 cups per feed per day.

Pour the required quantity of milk in a pot and heat it on a stove. Never use a microwave for heating the milk since the nutritional value is lost if milk is heated in a microwave. Keep your fingers in all the time while heating the milk since the milk boils very fast. Do not overheat the milk.

The temperature should be equivalent to the body temperature of the goat, that is, about 104 degrees. Milk should neither be chilly nor too hot but should be comfortably warm. Milk should be heated a little more if it is cold outside.

Milk can be poured into the bottle using a funnel or if multiple kids are being fed then the milk can just be poured into the bottle.

The nipple should be put onto the bottle. Once the baby goats are able to suck strong enough to bring it up to the tubes, nipples are put on to the feeder.

For older kids all you have to do is just show them the bottle and they will hold on and empty the bottle. New born kids who are being weaned and shifted to bottle feeding would need more training.

Rinse the nipples, bottles or the feeding equipment immediately in cold water after feeding. After rinsing in cold water wash them with warm soapy water. If feeding equipment is used then ensure to wash the tubes with tube wash at least once a week or more if necessary.

There a few tools to make feeding many kids easier namely:
- Multi-kid Feeder:

Advantages:
- Can be easily hung from a wall
- Kids are comfortable with the nipple
- Easy to clean

Disadvantages:
- Feeder cannot be used even if one piece is lost since it leaks
- Kids can push around so cannot really be secure when hung from a wall
- You cannot use nipples on bottles
- There are too many parts for instance ring seals, inner nipple holder, outer screw on ring
- It can feed only 6 kids each time

- Lam-Bar feeder

Advantages
- Can feed as many as 16 kids at a time
- Feeds fast
- Can be made at home
- Nipples can be replaced at a low cost and the tubes are easily available and economical
- Holder can be placed on the board on which the kids stand so that they can feed on without spilling
- You can use the nipples on bottles

Disadvantages
- It is a little hard to clean the feeder since the tubes have to be cleaned with a special brush at least once a week. If tubes are rinsed immediately after feeding then a brush is to be used

only once a week. If the tubes are not rinsed immediately then a brush has to be used every time.

- It is harder for the smaller kids to draw the milk up the straw. It is easier for some to get the milk up the straw but some require more time.

If you find it difficult to get the baby goat to take the bottle there are a few tips you could follow. Keep the baby goat on your lap. Place the bottle under your chin and bend down and rub the head of the baby with your chin and use your free hand to tickle the back of the baby goat. This will stimulate them to look for milk. It will be easier if two people can do it simultaneously. For instance if one of them is holding the bottle under the chin and rubbing the head of the baby with the chin the other person can tickle the back. On the other hand, while you are rubbing the head with the chin you can use the free hand to guide the nipple to the mouth of the baby goat.

How many times should you feed baby goats?

This really depends upon the age of the baby. When they are just born, you can give them as much food as they want. It is a good idea to feed them at least every 4 hours until they are one week old. Ideally, they will drink about 4 cups of milk each day.

After a week, you can reduce the frequency of feeding to 3 times each day. Once early in the morning, once in the afternoon and once just before you turn in. Even at this age they should not be given more than 4 cups each day. Although your goats may seem like they want a lot more, most often, they are just thirsty. So, keep some warm water available for them always.

You must mix equal portions of all the ingredients. Only the corn, soft white wheat and winter wheat must be increased to two and three portions respectively. Store them in an airtight container to keep them fresh.

After one month, you must reduce the feeding to twice a day. Divide the four cups into two portions. By the time they are about 3 months old, they are ready to consume hay and it is a good idea to wean them off the milk.

Feeding adult goats

You must always stock up on the food supplies to ensure that you don't compromise on the nutrition of your goats. It is true that goats will eat just about anything. In fact, you must allow them to forage around and graze. This is a very important part of their natural behaviour. However, if you are housing a herd or even pet goats, you must control their diet to an extent to make sure that they are healthy.

Grazing adds a lot of supplements to your goats diet, no doubt. Just like any other animal in their family, goats love to eat woody weeds, bushes and trees. They will also taste a bit of everything. However, this must be controlled as much as you can as grazing puts the goats at the risk of consuming harmful parasites. So, you must feed them enough to make sure that they do not graze too often.

Goats need certain important nutrients in order to produce good products like milk. For those who are interested in showing the goats, you must be extra careful with what you feed the goat. You must not allow the quality of the hair to reduce or even allow your goat to become obese.

Here are some recommended food options for goats:

Alfalfa and hay

If you live in an area where there are significant non grazing seasons, hay and alfalfa can become the main source of nutrients for your goats. Hay or alfalfa provide the goats with protein and a good dose of energy. Alfalfa is called legume hay and is more beneficial to your goat's health. In addition to high amounts of protein, they also contain calcium, vitamins and other minerals.

You must provide your goats with specially stored and cured hay for best results.

On an average, a goat will require about 4 pounds of hay every day. You should either make it available all day or make sure that the goats are fed twice each day even when the goats are browsing.

You also get alfalfa pellets that you can mix with the grains. This makes it easy to store and also reduces wastage.

Chaffhaye

Chaffhaye is a great substitute for grass hay. You can use early grass or alfalfa to make this. All you need is to chop the grass or alfalfa, spray with some molasses and add store bought culture of bacillus subtillis. Then, you need to vacuum pack the mixture. This hay will ferment in the bag. The bacterial culture that you add aids digestion in goats.

This is a great source of minerals, vitamins and energy. On an average, an adult goat will need about 2 pounds of chaffhaye for every 100 pounds in body weight. The nutritional value of 50 pounds of chaffhaye is equal to 100 pounds of high quality hay.

Grains

Pellet grain mixes or grains are great for your goat's diet. They provide minerals, vitamins and proteins. You can even give your goat store bought grain pellets that are formulated specially to provide nutrition to goats. These are the grain options that you can choose from:

- Whole grain: this includes unprocessed seed heads of grains.
- Pelleted grain: these products are made from whole grains or grain by-products that are broken into smaller pieces and then bound into pellets using a special agent.
- Rolled grain: Rolled grain is similar to whole gain. It is different in shape and is flat because it has been rolled.

- Texturized grain: This is similar to the previous option. The difference is that there are other ingredients that have been mixed with it to improve the health benefits.

Besides these regular foods, you must also provide your goats with supplements and medicated feed. This is extremely important if you are commercially rearing goats. You will also have to find good supplements if you have a pregnant doe or even an unwell goat at home.

Supplements for goats

You need to add supplemental vitamins, minerals and several other nutrients in the diet of your goats to keep them healthy. The most essential nutrients are vitamins and minerals. They are necessary for growth, for the development of strong skin and bones and to assist them when they are about to give birth.

There are loose minerals that you can provide as free choice. You may also choose to give your goats mineral blocks. You can find these in almost all pet stores. It is good to provide minerals with salt. If the mineral blocks available are salt free, you may have to add a salt block.

Avoid supplements that are labelled "goat/ sheep minerals". These are always low in copper. It is better to use horse minerals or regular cattle minerals instead.

There are some natural supplemental options that you can give your goats too. Some of the most recommended ones are:

Beet Pulp: It is rich in fiber and protein and is also a source of energy. It also contains traces of calcium and phosphorous that is great for the goats. It is best to purchase the 50 pound bags available in stores.

BOSS: Black oil sunflower seeds (BOSS) provide zinc, iron, vitamin E and selenium along with fat and fiber. These supplements add shine to the goats skin and also improve the butterfat content of the milk. You can just mix these seeds with the grains.

Kelp Meal: This is a good source of iodine and selenium. It reduces the chances of iodine deficiency in goats. This supplement also increase production of dairy including richness of milk and volume of milk produced.

Baking Soda: Several goat owners I know provide baking soda as a free choice mineral to goats. This is useful in improving their digestion and also maintains the pH of the rumen.

Apple Cider Vinegar: ACV contains several enzymes, minerals and vitamins that are useful for goats. You can just add the ACV to your goat's water.

Treats: Any pet loves treats. There are many snacks that are packed with nutrients, including:

- Corn chips that are excellent for the wethers because of the high saltiness. This makes them drink more water, preventing chances of calculi in the urine.

- Apples, watermelons, peaches, bananas, grapes and dried fruit are among the favorites of goats. Give them small pieces of these organic fruits to prevent choking.

- Vegetables like carrots, lettuce, pumpkin, spinach and any greens work really well with the goats.

What not to feed them

Of course, like all pets, even goats can be harmed by feeding them certain things. Many breeders and vets will encourage you to feed your pets with table scraps. Of course, that is alright as long as you know what you are putting into the tummy of your goat.

Pet owners often get so attached to their pets that they begin to treat them like they are part of the family. Yes, that is a good thing as long as you do not treat your pet like humans, in the anatomic sense. You see, the digestive tract of your goat is not designed to process all the foods that you consume. So, some things that you might consider extremely healthy for your family can actually ruin the health of your goats. In some cases, it may even kill your pet.

Here are some foods that you must avoid entirely when it comes to goats:

- Potatoes, tomatoes or any foods with alkaloids. They can be poisonous.
- Avocadoes
- Azalea
- African Rue
- Boxwood
- Brouwer's Beaut
- Burning bush berries
- Calotropis
- China Berry, all parts
- Choke Cherry
- Cassava
- Dumb Cane
- Datura
- Dog Hobble
- False Tansy
- Fusha
- Flizweed
- Holly
- Japanese Yew
- Japanese pieris
- Lakspur
- Lantana
- Lasiandra
- Lilacs
- Lily of the Valley
- Lupine
- Monkwood

- Maya maya
- Milkweed
- Mountain Laurel
- All Nightshade plants
- Rhubarb leaves
- Wild Cherry
- Tu Tu
- Yew

If you find any of these plants growing in your home, you must pluck them out. However, if you have planted them by choice, you must make a mesh or a fencing around the plant to prevent your goats from eating it.

These foods must always be avoided to ensure that your goats are healthy and developing properly.

2. Grooming your goat

If you are just raising goats on a farm as part of your green lifestyle, grooming them is not that essential. On the other hand, if you are looking at showing your goat at exhibitions and animal shows, you must pay closer attention to grooming.

In any case, you must include a few grooming routines as part of your goats daily care as there are some advantages like:

- The goat remains healthy
- You can check your goat for parasites
- Blood circulation improves
- Makes the goat comfortable with handling

There are some basic grooming routines that you must include. We will discuss some of them in more detail in the following sections. This is just a checklist to give you the basic idea.

Brushing: This is one of the most beneficial grooming routines, as it can remove any loose hair or dandruff. That helps improve the quality of your goat's skin and coat. The circulation of blood also increases and you can check for any signs of illness such as swelling, lumps or abscesses.

It is recommended to brush goats during early summer or late spring when they actually begin to shed the undercoat that they needed during winter. You will get special firm bristled brushes in pet stores.

When you brush the goat, start from the neck and move down the back and sides. Then, do not forget to brush the abdomen, chest and neck of your goat.

Bathing: Bathing goats is not required frequently. However, you can bathe your goats, especially if you are keeping them indoors, in order to avoid lice. Clipping the hair also becomes much easier when you bathe the goats. While warm water is recommended, there is no real harm in using cold water. You must use a goat shampoo or any animal shampoo.

When you are bathing the goat, kid or adult, make sure it is fastened with a harness. Then, you need to wet the body, lather up with the shampoo and then rinse thoroughly. Blow drying is only recommended if you plan to clip the hair immediately.

Clipping: Clipping your goats annually is a great idea. If the hair is shorter, the goats are able to stay cooler. There is also more sunlight on their skin, keeping lice and other parasites at bay. The best time to clip your goat's hair is a day or two after winter is fully over.

Most goat owners recommend two areas for clipping frequently:
1. The tail prior to kidding: Before and after the birth of a kid, there are several fluids that get stuck to the tail of the doe and the area around it. So, clip up the sides of the tail all the way to the end of the tail to make it short.

2. Udder: Make sure you remove the hair on the belly and around the udder. This is important to make sure that the hair does not fall into the milk.

Trimming the hooves: This is the least expensive goat care process. It is also the most important one. When you trim the hooves regularly, the health of your goat improves tremendously.

3. Clipping goat hair

Clipping your goat's hair annually is extremely beneficial to the animals. It also reduces the maintenance efforts on your part. An annual clip is best recommended as it helps keep the hair of the goats short enough for the rest of the year.

There are battery powered and electrical clippers that are available in most pet stores. If you are using these electrical clippers, you need to make sure that you check them frequently to ensure that they are not too hot. You will also have to spray the goat's body with water or cooling oil as required. The clippers need to be cleaned and piled as needed.

It is easier to clip the goat's hair if you wash the goat just before you clip the hair. This also increases the life of your clipper. If your clipper has dull blades, you need to be careful as it may irritate the goat. Many doe owners like to clip off the beard. However, clipping any area on the face is recommended only if you are planning to sow your goat. Otherwise, it is a real challenge.

You can follow these steps to trim your goat properly:

Secure the goat: you may use a harness. If it is a baby goat, you can just hold it. You can even keep some grain nearby to distract the goat.

Start from the top: When you are trimming the body of the goat, it is a good idea to use a 10 blade trimmer. Start from the top of the body and start trimming against the fur of your goat. Next, you need to use smooth and long motions to make sure that the hair doesn't look choppy and chunky. You need to move the skin over the hip and other bony areas to make sure that the cut is smooth.

The back and sides: Next you need to clip the hair from the neck, leg, chest, back and sides. The best way is to clip the areas with longer hair first and then move to the areas with shorter hair. If you want to correct the trimming, you can just move the trimmer with short strokes.

The belly and udder: When you are trimming the hair on the udder and belly, you need to be really careful. Use a 30 to 40 blade trimmer for this. Clip the middle of the belly till the area between the legs. Then when you are clearing the area around the udder, lift the legs and do so. As you clear the udder, hold the teats between your thumb and two fingers to make sure you don't nick the area.

Clear the hair above hooves: You would have noticed hair that is hanging over the hooves. Make sure you trim this hair.

Brush off the excess hair: To add the finishing touch, brush off any excess hair and then trim any uneven areas.

After you have finished clipping the hair of your goat, if you notice any area that is very exposed, you can rub some corn starch over it to avoid sunburns.

4. Trimming the hooves

Trimming the hooves of your goat can be really beneficial to the health of your goat. Several veterinarians recommend this as a way to increase your goat's life span.

Hooves often have a condition called hoof rot that you need to prevent by trimming the hooves regularly. Hoof rot starts of as a black lump on the sides of the hoof and then spreads to the entire hoof. Also, since the hooves can harbour several damaging parasites, making sure that they are clipped and maintained well can keep your goats healthy and also reduce unwanted vet bills for you.

The main purpose of hoof trimming is to make sure that the surface is even so that the goats can walk comfortably. Also, you don't leave any nooks and crannies for dirt to accumulate.

You will get special hoof trimmers at stores with cattle feed and supplies. You need to use this instrument to get a clean trim. You will also get an entire kit that consists of things like a hoof pick.

Here are a few simple tips to trim the hooves of your goat:

- First, clean the hooves thoroughly. You can use a hoof pick or even the edges of the trimmer.

- Then, trim the hoof slowly till you can see the pink area. If you go beyond this pink area, the goats will bleed. When you are trimming the front hooves, rest your shoulder against the body of the goat. Then, turn the leg back at the hinge of the knee and trim. When you are trimming the hind legs, you must sit behind the goat. Secure the leg at your armpit for maximum control.

- If there is any excess growth between the heel area, you need to trim that.

- Sometimes, you may see dirty pockets on the wall of the hoof, you must trim it completely. This pocket needs to be clean and open. If you leave the dirt pocket, you increase chances of hoof rot.

How do you know when trimming is needed
- Ideally, you must trim the hooves at least four times every year. Sometimes, you may have to do it a few more times. Usually, if your goats are allowed to play on rocky surfaces, they don't need trimming that often.

- It is easy to identify when your goat needs trimming. Check the back feet always. Usually, the front hooves are quicker to wear off and you may miss the trimming needs of the back hooves.

When you are trimming the hooves of your goat, you are aiming at getting a clean and even surface. It is a good idea to wash the hoof thoroughly with soapy water and scrub the surface well. This will make your job of trimming much easier.

You must also secure the goat well to ensure that there are no jerks or sudden movements that may lead to nips and cuts. So, you must tie them to a milk stand and also place some grains or feed to distract the animal.

5. The daily care checklist

Daily care for goats must be extremely methodical. Forgetting even the slightest detail can affect the health of your goats. So to make it easier for first time pet owners here is a quick checklist that you can use.

Checking the goats

- Count your herd every day.
- Do they look well or are they slow and lethargic?
- Do they sleep the right way?
- Do they seem anxious or scared?
- Is the poop abnormal?

Checking the shelter

- Has the door been tampered with?
- Can you see signs of shoe marks or scratches on the door?
- Can you see any loose slates that may fall off easily?
- Do you see droppings of another bird or animal besides your goats?
- Do you see any signs of red mite invasion?
- Are there any leaks?
- Is the ventilation okay?
- Is the floor area secured?
- Is the water clean?

- Is the feeder full?

Checking the property

- Can you see signs of a fox trying to dig in?
- Do you see fox droppings around the shelter?
- Are there any branches that the fox could jump in from?
- Is the fencing completely secure?
- Have you shut the gate?

These pointers are extremely important as they put the goats at risk. Keeping the door or the gate open is the cause for most deaths in a herd. It is very easy for predators to make their way into your home and harm the animals. I cannot state with complete confidence that these are the only precautions you need to take. There are several reasons why goats fall sick or even get eaten by predators. As the goat owner you need to be extremely vigilant if there is even single death in your herd. Put in all the efforts possible to find out the reason for fatalities to ensure that it does not extend to the rest of the herd.

6. Seasonal care for goats

Depending on the weather conditions and the temperatures in your area the kind of care you will take will vary greatly. The requirements of any pet are different in hotter months and different in the cooler months. Here are some things that you need to take care of during the summer and winter months respectively.

Summer care for goats

Most goat owners build two shelters for their goats. The more open ones are for the summer months and there are secure and closed ones for the winter. In case you do not have the facility to keep the goats in separate shelters for each season, you must take care to build the shelter where there is ample shade. This is usually under a tree or in an area where there is a large hedge.

If you let the goats range freely you will notice that their favourite spots are around the hedges and the bushes. There are several other points that you need to make sure of besides providing shade for your goats during the summer months.

• The shelter needs to be airy. Therefore, keep the vents clean and open. Most often, goats like to sleep outdoors during the warmer months. So, you may have to build a secure fence around the shelter with ample space outside for the goats to sleep and rest.

• When you have a large herd, it is also advisable to use a fan or an industrial cooler inside the shelter if it gets too hot. Make sure that the goats are not able to reach the fan.

• Clipping the hair of your goat during the summer months is an excellent idea as it helps the animals stay cooler.

• Make sure that there is enough water available for your goats during the warmer months. This is the most important thing to prevent any deaths from dehydration.

The good news about summer maintenance is that it is much easier than a winter month. Cleaning the shelter is just 1/3rd the work that is required than the colder months. The only thing you need to worry about during the hot months is the mite issues. So make sure that you inspect the shelters regularly and check every nook and cranny. In case you witness any mites just use an eco-friendly powder that can be sprinkled in the areas that are infected to keep the area clean.

Winter care for goats

Many goat owners neglect the importance of winter care for goats under the assumption that the animals grow an undercover anyway. Yes, this is their natural way of staying warm. However, if you are experiencing very severe winters, you must take certain precautions to ensure that your goats are completely healthy even during the colder months. In many cases, goats have developed pneumonia because their winter care was neglected.

Here are some tips for winter care of your goats:

Preparing the shelter: The first thing you need to ensure is that your goat's housing area has a door or covering. This will block any cold drafts from entering the enclosure. It will also prevent any influx of moisture.

Heating: It is a good idea to use a heating lamp. However, you need to be extra cautious. Several barn fires have started because of heaters that were not controlled well. The lamp must never come in contact with the bedding as the dry bedding can catch fire easily.

Sleeping arrangements: Make the floor warm with bedding material like pine shavings and hay. During the colder months, goats prefer to sleep on a raised platform. So, you may consider installing sleeping shelves for your goat. You must also fluff and rotate the bed occasionally to ensure that it is not damp.

Warming the goats: Usually, goats develop an undercoat during winter. However, if your goat is unwell or if it belongs to a breed that cannot develop an undercoat, you may want to use readymade goat coats. They are available in pet stores and are made from fleece.

With these precautions, you can be sure that your goats remain healthy, irrespective of the temperature and the climate outside. They will be active and also productive when they are cared for properly.

Caring for Senior Goats

When you have an aging goat on your farm, there may be certain issues you face, especially if you are trying to raise a flock:

- Poor health due to improper nutrition
- Lack of productivity that leads to unnecessary maintenance costs.
- Eventual death due to old age.

Usually, most goat owners consider their goats to be seniors when they are about 12 years old. You will observe a change in the behaviour and in the normal routine of the goat when it is old. The first sign is that they are less aggressive and in case of the does, them my slowly become unproductive.

Now, if you are looking at a business with these goats, the best option is to cull them from the rest of the herd. This means that you will separate the old and unproductive goats and rear them separately. The advantage of culling is that the carrying costs of your flock are greatly reduced. When you cull the older goats, there will be no wastage of quality feed for the high yielding goats.

Also, with the increase in demand for goats as pets, when you cull the unproductive goats, you will find that their market value does not reduce drastically.

However, you must be very careful with what you feed your older goats. Since they are less active, they tend to become fat or obese quite easily. An obese goat is a goat with health issues, and therefore, a goat with high vet bills.

The proportion of feed is extremely important when it comes to aging goats. It is recommended that you feed an aging goat about 6% of his body weight every day.

Aging goats will forage and browse. While that is necessary for them, you must also make sure that you provide the goat with a well balanced diet plan. Make sure that the diet is rich in fiber. This allows easy digestion. You may include beet pulp along with hay or alfalfa when you are feeding your senior goat to make up for the fiber requirements.

You may also add a mineral block in the barn of your senior goats to make up for their mineral requirements. If the goats are being given grains, you might want to add about 14 to 16 % of proteins in the form of calf starters or protein blocks that are available in stores.

Senior goats also require continuous access to fresh food. If you can maintain this, you will be able to give your senior goats a healthy life.

7. Putting a pet to rest

Eventually, you will have to deal with the death of your goats. Goats may die due to old age or due to health issues. Sometimes, still births may also occur in your barn. As painful as it is to deal with the death of a pet, you must make sure that you dispose the carcass properly, to honor your pet and to protect the others from any disease that the dead animal may be harbouring. Here are some ways of putting your pet to rest:

Burial

This is the most common and the most inexpensive way to dispose of a dead goat. The animal is buried in a deep pit that is 4 to 6 feet deep. Find a spot that is safe from rain water or loose soil. That way leaching will not occur. Although this method works well for pet owners, it may not be the best way for a person interested in raising a flock. Of course, there is always some chance of scavengers reaching the carcass as well. Burying frequently also leads to soil or water contamination.

Incineration

This is the most effective way to deal with the carcass as all the pathogens will be destroyed. However, incinerators can only dispose goats that weigh less than 60 pounds, usually. In addition to that, it is expensive to buy and run an incinerator.

Composting

This has become a popular method on farms. The body is decomposed by aerobic bacteria into a nitrogen rich compound that makes a great organic fertilizer. This method also destroys all the pathogens.

Large compost pits containing saw dust are installed on the property. They can be turned regularly to reduce the carcass into usable compost in a couple of weeks.

These are the most recommended and the most popular methods used by pet owners to put their beloved pets to rest.

If your pet is terminally ill

If you have a goat that is very sick, it is best to put him to rest if you have tried all measures to help him. This is because not only does the animal become an added expense, it may also spread the disease to the entire herd.

You can choose on-farm euthanasia or you could seek the assistance of your vet.

On farm: A captive bolt gun or a gunshot is used to euthanize the animal. This requires expertise as you must shoot the animal at an exact spot near the temporal region of the head. You must also be able to effectively determine whether the animal is dead before disposing the carcass.

By the vet: Vets can administer an anaesthesia overdose. This is undoubtedly the most humane way to put an ailing animal to rest.

Euthanizing the animal should be your last option. Personally, the gunshot seems a little far-fetched, although it is a popular method globally.

Chapter 10: Interacting With Your Goats

1. Understanding goat behavior

Goats are capricious creatures. This means that they are extremely whimsical and quite comical at times. However, you must never underestimate the capacities of your goats. They are curious creatures and are extremely intelligent.

Goats are often considered to be very aloof and unloving. But this, in my opinion is the biggest myth as far as goats are concerned. They are really loving creatures who love to play and be around people.

However, you need to understand that your goat is nothing like the dog you have at home. Unlike dogs, goats are not looking for your approval. They will be attached to you, no doubt, but they are going to behave just like any other goat and not worry about you being pleased with them.

So, if you are expecting your goat to jump up onto your lap, I would hate to bust your fairytale expectations. Nevertheless, goats are wonderful pets and give you several opportunities to interact with them and play with them. However, for them to get comfortable around you, you need to be able to understand their behavior. That is when you can create a sense of trust between you and your goat.

What you need to understand also is that the behavior of goats changes rather drastically from the time when they are kids to the time that they become mature. The only way you can familiarize yourself with goat behavior is by spending enough time with your goats. That way, you will also be able to understand herd behavior along with individual goat behavior properly.

Behavior of kids

Like any baby, goat kids will also learn all their behaviour patterns from their mother and from the older members of the herd. If you are raising bottle fed kids, you need to make sure that they interact with the existing herd.

If you fail to do this, the kids will not learn simple things like browsing or eating grain. They will also look for a bottle for their food. That will make them disinterested in other foods, thereby compromising their health significantly.

Even if you are bottle feeding kids, you must make sure that they are with the herd from the first day. You must bring a kid indoors only if it is weak or if it is being fed through tubes. Usually, mothers may reject a kid which leads to bottle feeding. However, he must still be allowed to interact with his mother and his siblings.

Here are some behavior patterns that you will find common among the kids in a herd:

Hiding or getting lost: This is something that goat kids are great at. They usually get into little holes and spaces where they can hide. Then, they sit there really quietly. This is a natural instinct that helps them survive in a herd. If there are any spaces on your property that could act as caves, you will most often find them hiding in these caves.

If you thought that the mother would be able to find her kids, you are seriously mistaken! Several studies over the years have found that kids are so good at hiding that even the moms can't find them. Most often, the mother would just wander away with no clue of where the kid is!

Several goat owners that I know have told me that they have been unable to locate kids for hours and sometimes overnight. Then they are found in the herd the next day or under a pile of things in a secluded corner.

To be prepared for this devious hiding, you may want to use brightly colored collars that will help you locate them easily.

Chewing: Undoubtedly, baby goats love to explore. Just like the babies of other species of animals, baby goats, too, love to explore with their mouths. So, they will chew on things and ruin them a little to learn more about them.

Climbing: Baby goats love to climb. In fact, they love to climb on their moms. This is allowed only with the mom and not with any other herd member. Essentially, a baby goat will climb only on members of the family. So, if you see a little kids trying to climb you, then, you should feel really privileged. Climbing is a baby goat's way of having a good time. They actually consider anything that they can climb as toys. This includes a fallen tree, logs, spools of cable, a picnic table and play forts that you can build for them.

Sneezing: This is a behaviour pattern that they will carry on into their adulthood. In goats, sneezing is not a sign of illness. It is actually a warning sign. If you see your goat sneezing, you must know that there is some danger (like a predator) lurking around. If the sneeze is not too tensed or alarmed, it could just be a part of a game.

Head Butting: Head butting among kids is quite different from head butting among adults. It is less aggressive and is usually playful. It is a good idea to help the kids practice head butting. If you gently push the head of a kid, he will push back. However, you must remember never to push the forehead. This is important especially if the goats are a little big. It may lead to an aggressive reaction that could be dangerous for you. When you push the forehead of a goat, you are threatening his position in the herd.

Behavior of adult goats

Among adult goats, all their behavior patterns are directed towards maintaining their position in a herd. Yes, they can be playful at times. However, the main agenda is to show their worth in a herd.

Another significant behavior change or pattern is when your goat is trying to send out signs that he is ready for mating or when she is nursing. Here are some common behavior patterns you can observe in adult goats:

Fighting and dominance: The herd dynamics in goats is ever changing. Every goat has the ability to attain the position of the top buck or the flock queen if he or she can fight it out. So, you will see fighting quite commonly among adult goats.

Fighting is pronounced when new goats are introduced into a herd. If you do not find any animal in danger, there is no need to intervene as this is natural for goats.

If a doe has kidded recently or if she is about to kid, she will try to improve her status in the herd. This is primarily an attempt to get her kids a better status. During these times, you cannot do much but let them fight it out even if it is too aggressive.

Goats also take sides when there is a fight. They tend to become helpers to the two goats who are in the main fight. The fights include several signs of aggression such as:
1. Hitting and ramming
2. Pawing
3. Blubbering
4. Leg pawning

Pawing: When a doe has just given birth to kids, she engages in pawing. This is her way of getting the kids to stand up and start moving around. If you think that she is attacking the kids, let me tell you that this is her way of showing that she cares!

However, you need to watch the pawing closely if you notice that the mother is very enthusiastic. In some cases, she may kill the kid accidentally.

This is not a sign of refusal either. When a mother refuses her new born, she will butt it or just ignore it.

Sexual behavior: Both does and bucks show similar reactions when they are in heat. Here are some signs that will tell you that your goat is in heat.
1. Tongue flapping: The buck will flap his tongue on the sides of the doe he is interested in. A buck may also initiate this behavior or reciprocate this way.
2. Leg pawing: Along with the tongue flapping the buck will also straighten his leg and paw the sides of the doe.
3. Blubbering

Urinating: Urinating is a sign of when the bucks go into heat or into a rut. You will notice that they spray on their front legs and on their faeces. Bucks actually have a special attachment on the genitalia to do this! He will even spray it into the mouth, curl up the lips and smell it. He does this to coat himself with his sticky urine that the does find attractive. A cologne for goats, I guess!

Developing an odor: You will notice that bucks begin to smell really bad as they grow. For some this smell is not exactly bad but is rather strong. The odor becomes worse with maturity. If you are interested in milking the does, keep them away from such bucks as the smell could creep into the milk.

Goats exhibit several other distinct herd and individual habits that you will need to get used to. You will become familiar with these habits as you observe your goats and interact with them.

2. Getting goats to behave well

In order to make your interactions with your goats more pleasant, it is a good idea to get them to learn a few manners. Yes, it is possible to train goats as they are intelligent, social animals.

When you train your goats well, they will also be easier to handle. That way, if your goat needs to be carried and taken to the vet, you will not have to fight it out, really.

Here are some tips to teach your goats how to behave well.

Use a collar

This is the best way to handle your goats. If you plan to show your goats, they are extremely essential. They help you lead a goat in and out of different places. You will also need a collar to handle your goat when you are grooming them.

If you have one or two goats, you can buy collars in stores. However, if you want to purchase collars for a large herd, you might want to place bulk orders in goat supply stores for discounts.

You may even use a regular dog collar. Make sure that you take the collar off when your goat is out in the open. This reduces the risk of choking or getting hooked some where.

Handle them regularly

If you do not handle your goats regularly, they will not be social and peaceful. When they become wild and unused to human company, they may even try to run away. So for all routine maintenance activities and while grooming, it is a good idea to handle your goats. You can train your goat only when you handle it regularly.

Here are some tips to handle goats:
- When goats try to escape, they usually try to get the head away. So, you must try to keep the head up at all times. For this you need to place a hand below the chin and the other one over the neck. Always be careful as you may choke the animal accidentally.

- If the goat is fleeing, always catch him by his back legs. If you try to grab the forelimbs, they may just break.

- Never chase a goat. Use treats or food to lure them instead.
- When you are handling your goat using the horns, the grip must be very firm.

- Before a visit to the vet, catch the goat well in advance and restrain it in a shelter.

Teach them manners

If you are able to teach your goat some basic manners, you will find it easier to interact with it. You will also see that training a goat that has been trained to behave well is a lot easier.

If your goats have horns, you must be particularly concerned about teaching him manners to keep him calm around visitors and to keep your visitors safe. Here are some tips to teach your goat manners:

- Never push the forehead of the goat. This stimulates aggression and makes the goat believe that it is okay to head butt people.

- Although kids can be allowed to climb you, you must always discourage jumping.

- Your goats must never be allowed to stand with its forelimbs on you. This is okay for dogs and not goats.

- Children must not be allowed to tease or ride the goats. This makes the goats fearful of all human company.

3. Training your goat

There is no doubt that you can train your goat to lead a comfortable life with people. Goats may not really play fetch unless you spend a lot of time on a single goat. Even then, expecting them to fetch is a little unrealistic. However, there are some training routines that can be of great help to your goats, such as:

Leash training your goat

You must train your goats to walk with a lead. This is essential not only when you are showing your goats but even on a regular basis in order to make it easier to handle the animals. You can follow the given points for about 10 minutes each day until the goat is familiar with the leash concept.

Use a collar: You need to first get the collar around the goat's neck. Make sure that the collar is not too tight or too loose. You don't want the goat to choke or slip off.

Attach the lead: Just like the dog, your goat also needs a collar that has been placed correctly to make the lead comfortable. Make sure that the lead fits near the top jaw and then comes up from behind the head.

Walk a few steps: Now you need to start leading the goat. Pull it gently and walk a few steps. If your goat walks with you, then reward it with a treat and shower praises. You can slowly increase the distance as the goat gets more uncomfortable. Never pull the leash too hard as the goat may suffocate and collapse.

Teach the goat to follow: Your goat must also learn to stop when you stop. So, use treats to encourage walking, making sure that the goat is always behind you. Whenever the goat walks past you, shout stop and turn to the opposite direction. When the leash stops the goat, wait and give him time to turn in your direction.

It will take some practice every day to get your goat accustomed to the leash. After each lesson, make sure you remove the lead and the collar and allow the goat to be with the herd.

Training a goat to pack

Once you have trained your goat to follow your lead, you can also take him with you on hikes. They are great for backpacking.

When you plan to take your goats on camps, they must be trained for the following:

- Your goats must get used to being tied. When you go on camps, the goats will be tied when you are resting. For this you will need a leash and a sturdy collar. Start by tying the goat to a fence and observing him. If he begins to get restless and if he tangles himself in the leash, just untangle him. As he gets used to this concept, increase the time that you keep him tied up for.

- Your goat must follow your lead. This will happen only when you leash train him completely.

- They must learn to stand as well. There will be several instances when your goats will have to stand during the trial. This means that your goat must learn to stop when you halt. This is possible only when he is trained regularly.

- They must also get used to wearing the pannier that they will carry stuff in. You can start by allowing the goat to examine the pannier. Then, saddle it on the back with a gap for two fingers between the body and the cinch strap of the saddle.

Advanced training for goats

As your goat is accustomed to interacting with you, you may teach him more complicated tricks. You need a lot of patience for this and you must spend several hours with your pet goats to be successful. There are two things with advanced training:

Using a clicker: Goats can be taught just about any trick in the book using a clicker. A clicker is a mechanical device that you will find in most pet stores. This device makes a long clicking sound and when combined with treats like peanuts, it is an excellent training aid.

The sound of the clicker with the treat tells the goat that he is doing something right. For this, you need to make that connection between the treat and the clicker. To establish this, make a sound with the clicker and give the goat a treat about 30 times. This will make the goat respond to the clicker as it would respond to a treat.

The next step is to start training the goat. Use a cue word such as "come". When the goat does what you expect it to, just click. If he completes the task, add a bonus and give him a treat.

The goat will learn to respond to commands with a lot of practice. When you are teaching more complicated tricks, break them down and teach each step using a clicker.

The obstacle course: If you want to show your goat, you must make sure that you teach him to complete an obstacle course. You can use a clicker and treats to train your goat.

When you create the obstacle course, be creative. Use steps, hoops and even old tires. Anything that the goat can climb or go through may be used.

4. Disbudding a goat

Disbudding is the process of removing the horns of a goat. It is always recommended to disbud baby goats or kids when the time is right. There are several goat owners who may find this practice rather unnatural and even unethical. However, for safety reasons, disbudding is recommended.

If your goats get aggressive, they can actually cause fatalities if they have not been disbudded. The horns can also get caught in fences and wires causing great distress to the animal. In case you are unsure about disbudding, you must at least file the tips of the horns to reduce the damage. If you want the goats to be completely natural, you can opt for breeds called polled breeds that do not have horns naturally.

Here are some advantages of disbudding a goat that you may want to consider before you reject this idea:

- Horned goats get stuck in fences and feeders. Sometimes, you may have to cut out a part of the fence to release the animal. A goat that is stuck is also more vulnerable to predator attacks. Goats that have horns are destructive. They have the habit of rubbing or banding their horns against hard surfaces, including fences and feeders. They may also harm you, your pet or other members of the herd. It may also injure visitors on your farm, making you liable.

- Most goat shows do not allow horned goats. So, these goats have a lower market potential.

- Milking a horned doe requires special milking stands with a lock for the head.

So, you see, disbudding has several advantages. However, if you feel like it is a cruel practice, it is a view that you are entitled to.

Disbudding a kid

It is always recommended that you disbud a goat when it is still a kid. Ideally, a kid must be disbudded within two weeks of birth. In case of males, the growth of the horns is faster, making it essential to disbud them when they are about 2 or 3 days old.

You must never wait for the goat to be a grown up to remove the horns. It is not as simple as just cutting the horns off as the horns contain large blood vessels. Cutting too low may actually rupture one of the blood vessels and cause profuse bleeding. Try to get a veterinarian to help you out. You can also take the assistance of an experienced friend who has had goats on the farm. You can do it yourself only when you are sure of doing this. You may use a disbudding iron to do this. Never ever use disbudding paste as it is a very inhumane way of disbudding the goat. When you are sure, you may use the following method to disbud your goat.

- Give your goat a tetanus shot. You will be able to find the syringe and the antibiotic in any pet pharmacy.

- Place the goat in a kid holder with the head sticking out of the rectangular area.

- Preheat your iron for about 20 minutes.

- In the meantime, use a clipper to clip the horn area till you can see the horn bud.

- Then, hold the head of the goat firmly with you hand placed below the muzzle. Apply the iron on the horn bud. You must apply some pressure and rock the iron from side to side for about 8 seconds. The head must not move an inch during this process.

- You know that the process is complete when you have two dry copper rings in the bud area.

Dealing with scurs

When the disbudding process is complete successfully, blood supply to the horn bud will be stopped, making them fall off after a while. However, sometimes the horn buds may grow back in the form of partial horns that are known as scurs. This is a common occurrence among bucks. To prevent scurs, some goat owners burn two circles at the horn bud. You must check for regrowth regularly. If you notice even the slightest growth, you must burn it again.

If the scur grows when the goat is too large to handle, just let it be. Chances are these scurs will fall off during a fight.

Scurs are not really an issue unless they are too large. When large scurs break, bleeding is profuse. Then, you need to spray blue Kote on the area to prevent any infection. If you are unsure about how to deal with a large scur, you must meet a vet. Otherwise, the scur can be harmful to people and other goats. In some cases the scurs curl and grow towards the eye. Then, you need to pad it to prevent any injury. If the growth towards the eye is too much, the horn needs to be cauterized by a vet.

Chapter 11: Identifying and Transporting Goats

If you are running a business with your goats, you will have to occasionally transport them. You may also have to take your goats out to visit the vet or even take them out with you when you are travelling. So, it is important to know the safest means to get your goats from one place to another. Basically, with identification marks, you can prove that a certain goat belongs to you when they are lost or even stolen.

In many states, registering goats and identification signs for them is mandatory. So, whether your state demands it or not, it is best that you choose this option anyway.

The first step towards ensuring the safety of your pets is to be able to identify them properly. Whether they run away from your property or are shipped wrongly, you need to be able to trace your goat. There are two popular methods mentioned below, that you can choose from.

1. Identifying your goats

You must be able to identify your goats whether you are just keeping them as pets or whether you are using them for a business. The truth about goats is that they can break away quite easily and can be difficult to find thereafter. Additionally, when you are occasionally transporting goats, you need to be sure that they have some identification mark to help you locate them. Here are two options that you have:

Tattooing

It is possible to tattoo a sequence of letters or numbers on your goat to help identify them. Tattooing requires you to register your animal with a local registry first. Then they will give you a tattoo

103

sequence or a registry sequence that you may use. There are also restrictions of the identification methods in some places. So, you must make sure that you check first.

The tattoo is usually made on the ears of the goat or on the tail web. You can seek professional assistance for this. However, there are some tattoo kits that you can get from supply stores as well. These kits contain the special ink and tattoo tongs that will help you make the marking.

It is tricky as pushing the tattoo tong in wrongly can damage the ear and also lead to immense bleeding. So, you must start off with someone experienced before you go on to do it yourself.

Microchipping

This method is more humane. However, it is a lot more expensive than tattooing. Microchips are available in the form of injectors. They resemble a large syringe. Within each syringe is a special number. You will also get several stickers with these numbers when you get a microchip for your goat. These chips are read with a special microchip reader.

Microchips are usually inserted into the tail web, on the left side. If you know how to inject the goat safely, you may do it yourself. Otherwise, it is recommended that you take the help of a veterinarian.

2. Containers you may use for transportation

When it comes to safe transportation, the first step is to find a container that your goat can be comfortable in. There are two options that are best suited for goats:

Plastic Tubs

Plastic transportation tubs are easy to make, and can often be created from recycled or repurposed materials, making them quite affordable. They are feasible when you are transporting kids or small goats. To transform a tub into a suitable transport option, simply drill several 1-inch holes on the top and sides of the tub to provide ventilation. By placing the holes in this manner, air will be drawn in through the sides and vented out through the holes in the lid.

Place some dry straw at the bottom of the tub to provide comfort and to absorb liquids.

If not properly ventilated, this type of transportation vessel can become very damp and full of polluted air that can make your goat very sick.

Opaque tubs are the best choice, as they will prevent the goats from seeing the activity outside the container. This can stress them, making them more susceptible to illness. Transparent containers can be used, but they should be covered with a lightweight covering to prevent the goats from becoming stressed.

Wire Cages

Wire cages are perhaps the most popular choice for transporting goats. These are available commercially in a variety of styles, sizes and price points. The other primary benefits of wire cages are that they offer plenty of ventilation for the inhabitants, which can make them more comfortable in warm environments. However, the open nature of the cage means that these are messier than plastic tubs and odors, spilled water, food and feces are likely to escape the boundaries of the cage from time to time. In cold weather, such cages cannot be left exposed to the elements for extended periods of time.

3. Transportation choices

Once you have chosen the container that you want to keep your goats in, you will have to choose the mode of transport. The mode of transport depends upon the distance that the goats will be travelling. Remember that any pet finds travelling rather stressful. So, if you plan to drive them for long distances, you must be prepared to have a really sick and upset goat in the back seat.

Usually, there are three transportation options that are available to pet owners:

Your Personal Vehicle

If you have a car or a truck you can transport your goats in them. It is important to have ample boot space when you plan to transport goats. Goats can get restless when they are being driven around. Also, they may have falls if they are not secured properly. This is something you need to be very careful about.

If you are transporting a goat for the first time, you might want to use a container. Make sure that the size is just right to prevent them from falling and hurting themselves. The bedding should be soft and thick to provide ample cushioning. You must also ensure that food and water is available to the goats. If you are transporting adult goats, you might want to carry them in separate carriages, unless they are from the same herd and are quite peaceful. If you are transporting multiple goats, make sure that they are able to see their companions so that they feel secure. While transporting goats, you must also try and keep them warm.

Some people also have trailers that they attach to their vehicles when they are frequently transporting goats.

Shipping

You may also use the postal services to transport your goats. If you are considering shipping your goats in overnight carriages, it is important for you to obtain a health certificate from a licensed veterinarian. This rule is applicable in most states. The certificate must be obtained at least 10 days prior to shipping.

The best option is the bio- safe carrier that is used to transport pets. These carriers come with a lining that is water resistant. They also have air holes to ensure oxygen supply to the animal.

It is advisable to take the package yourself to the airport that the goats will fly out of. Your local post office will be able to give you that information. Make sure that the flight is non-stop. This will reduce travel stress for your goats. If you must make a stop, ensure that the second half of the journey is covered by road or rail.

Make sure that your carrier screams out that there are live animals in it. Although there are signs on the packages usually, you must ensure that you highlight this fact. This is because any live animal is treated differently from other cargo. They are transported in areas that are safe and comfortable.

It is a good idea to line the box with warm bedding. You must also make sure that the material you use gives the goat proper foothold to prevent injuries due to skidding.

Shipping goats in the beginning of the week is ideal as the staff remains the same. If you ship them anytime after Thursday, there is a higher possibility of mix ups. Shipping or air travel should be the last option when you are transporting your goats. If you can avoid it, make sure you do to avoid unnecessarily traumatizing the animals.

Estimated Costs.

The cost of shipping goats, like any other shipment, depends entirely on the size of the package. Usually, a package will have weight restrictions. Additionally, if you are shipping them beyond zone 5, the costs will go up. However, if you are sending the shipment to zone 5 or beyond, the cost will not change much with weight.

Another added expense is when you request for express mail. There is a $10-$15 (£6 -10) additional charge with express mail. Usually animals are sent via Priority mail. The truth is that the time taken by priority mail and express mail is almost the same. There is no real difference.

The shipping costs include:

- The kennel
- A health certificate, if required

- Ground transport, if required

All in all, you will spend about $80/ £100 for the shipping itself. In addition to that you will pay $50/ £30 for the box and the supplies necessary to ensure a safe trip for your goats.

4. Safety Regulations

Regardless of the type of transportation vessel you use, always be sure that the container is securely strapped into your vehicle, by using seatbelts, bungee cords or straps. In addition to keeping your goats safer in the event of an accident, it will help prevent the container from sliding around – something that can cause you to have an accident in the first place!

Never leave goats unattended in a hot car. The glass windows create a greenhouse effect, which can cause the internal temperature to rise to dangerous levels very quickly. Goats can and have died from being left in a hot car.

Avoid playing loud music or driving erratically while chauffeuring your goats. Ultimately, a car ride can be a very stressful experience and you should try to keep the event as stress-free as possible.

Chapter 12: Breeding, Kidding and Milking

If you decide to bring home a herd of goats, you must also be prepared to meet all the breeding requirements of your animals. In case you have a pregnant doe, you must also provide proper care. When you have kidded a doe, you must also be aware of all the special requirements of a new born kid. This includes vaccinations and proper nutrition for both the mother and the baby.

1. Preparing your goats for breeding

You must be familiar with specific goat behavior if you are interested in breeding them. The maturity of the goat is the most important thing with goats. Usually goats can be bred when they are about 4 to 6 months old. As for the does, the safest time to breed them is when they are 7 months old. That way, you will be able to kid the doe when she is 1. If your goat is underweight or underdeveloped, you may want to consult your vet before breeding.

Usually, goats breed in the fall. When the breeding season starts, you need to start taking precautionary measures such as improving food quality and living conditions to ensure that the goats are at optimal health when they are ready to breed. You must try to avoid handling the bucks during this season as they have a terrible odor. To make sure you don't get the smell all over you, here are some tips you must follow:

- Give the goats a BoSe dose
- Trim the hooves
- Clip the hair on the belly of the bucks
- Test the goats for CAEV
- Have a fecal analysis done
- Deworm the goats

There are certain mating rules that goats follow. So, it is natural for them to exhibit behaviors like butting, pawing, blubbering and also snorting. The bucks and does have their roles figured out, which means that you don't have too much to worry about.

Breeding among goats is seasonal. There are certain breeds that can be bred all year long. However, they will experience maximum heat during the fall season. If you live close to the equator, then the heat may not be seasonal.

Towards early fall, the daylight decreases. This is a clear indication for the does to go in to their estrus or heat. This period ends with ovulation. From the month of July until January, does will go into heat almost every month or even every three weeks. There may be some short cycles during the initial period of the breeding season. This is when the goats will come into heat earlier than 3 weeks or a month.

The short cycle is alright in the beginning. These cycles are 18 to 24 days long. However, if the short cycles persist, they could be an indication of cysts on the ovary. This means that the goat is less likely to conceive. She must be given medication to break the cyst.

When the males notice the decreased daylight, they go into, what is called, a rut. During that period, the only thing on their mind is mating. So they will get into fights, not rest, stay up for long hours and not eat properly. As the days get shorter, the hormones will kick in making your goats a lot more restless and uneasy. It is a good idea to start planning breeding as per your schedule.

The normal gestation period for a goat is 5 months.

2. The ABC of goat breeding

There are three things that you need to prepare yourself for when you want to breed your goats:

A: The does in heat

You must know whether your doe is ready for breeding or not. It is easier to tell with mature goats, in comparison to the kids. Here are some signs that you must watch out for:

- Redness and swelling in the vulva
- Vaginal discharges
- A vigorous tail wagging exercise called flagging
- Very loud calls that range from short bleats to really long ones.
- Parading or walk back and forth a buck that is also in heat
- They will behave like bucks and mount other goats. This way, other goats can mount her. They will also get into fights.
- Does focus mostly on attracting the bucks and are not really interested in food. So, milk production is reduced. You can also blame the hormonal changes for this.

B: The buck in a rut

When the bucks are in a rut, they can do some rather ugly things to attract the opposite gender. Some common things you will notice are:

- Urination on the chest face and beard
- Blubbering
- Snorting
- Grunting
- Making a face by curling the upper lip
- Fighting
- Mounting to show dominance

It is common for a buck to mate 20 times a day. This is quite stressful for them. As a result, they lose their appetite and will also lose weight over a period of time. So, it is important to supplement your buck's feed with beet pulp, leaves and grains.

C: The act of breeding

It is a good idea to put the doe with a buck when you notice that she is in heat. Naturally, the buck will be very interested. He will show his approval by stomping and pawing with his forelimbs. If the doe urinates, the buck will put his nose into it.

As for the doe, she will flag her tail rapidly. When the buck mounts her, she will stand still. Foreplay may be in the form of circling each other.

The actual coitus is only for a few seconds. They must engage in the act at least three times to make sure that the doe is pregnant. In case that the doe does not come back to heat, it is a sign that it was successful.

In very rare cases, the doe will dislike a buck. That time she will do anything to get away. It is common for older does to reject younger bucks.

In case the does and bucks have been living together during the breeding season, you will have to make a separate shelter when the kids arrive. He can be a pain when the doe is in labor or may re breed the doe prematurely.

3. Complications during pregnancy

When you have a pregnant doe, you must take extra care. You must make sure that she is checked by the vet regularly. You must also keep her isolated to prevent her from getting any infections or spreading any infections in the herd. You must also provide supplements and high quality feed to ensure that she is able to meet all her nutritional requirements. Despite all these precautions, there are some complications that may occur when the doe is pregnant.

You must also watch out for false pregnancy. When this happens, the doe will show all the signs of pregnancy which include:

- An enlarged udder

- Uterine cramping

However, pregnancy tests may be negative. This is caused by a
uterine infection. The phase will end with a cloudburst which
is the release of a large amount of fluid. This is not a
complication and the doe will go back to normal.

The complications that may occur are:

Abortion

Abortion or sometimes still birth can be caused due to:

- A kid that is not formed properly. Such kids will have genetic
disorders and will be naturally aborted in the beginning of the
gestation.

- Stress due to overcrowding, poor diet or extreme weather
conditions.

- An infectious disease. We will discuss the diseases in detail in
the next chapter.

- Poisoning due to plants or medication

- Injury from fights or accidents.

Hypocalcemia

This condition occurs towards the end of the pregnancy. It may
also occur when the goat is lactating. If you have a dairy goat,
hypocalcemia is common. The symptoms include:

- Loss of appetite
- Progressive weakness
- Depression
- Low temperature
- Lethargy

You will notice that your doe is particularly averse to grains. This condition can only be prevented by managing the diet of the goat when she is pregnant or lactating. It is a good idea to feed her with alfalfa for calcium. Reduce the grain consumption or break in into several meals.

If the goat is consuming a lot of grain and alfalfa during her lactation, continue this cycle for the whole pregnancy.

If the goat is bred when she is dry, grain or alfalfa is not recommended until the last two months of pregnancy.

If your doe has hypocalemia, you need to give her 60ml of proplylene glycol each day. You can also contact your vet to give her CMPK which is a dose of calcium, magnesium, phosphorous and potassium.

Ketosis

This is common if the doe is overweight at the beginning of pregnancy. You will notice a sweet smelling breath in the doe if she has ketosis. She may also show some symptoms of hypocalcemia.

You can treat the goat similar to the way to treat her for hypocalcemia.

4. How to prepare for kidding

It is very essential that you prepare well in advance for the kidding process to make sure that it goes on smoothly. You must prepare the doe and also prepare for the extra member that will now become part of your herd.

You must begin a routine care towards the last two months of pregnancy. Here are some things you can do to ensure optimal health for your goat when she is about to give birth:

- If the area that you live is low in selenium, you must give the doe a BoSe shot that gives her a dose of Vitamin E. This should be done 5 weeks before the expected date of delivery. This can prevent abnormal labor, helps the placenta pass easily and reduces the chance of white muscle disease in the kids.
- A shot of CDT toxocid vaccine is recommended four weeks before the kidding date. This will make the kids more immune to enterotoxemia and tetanus.
- The tail and udder area should be trimmed so that the kidding is more hygienic. It will also make it easier to nurse the kids as they will be able to reach the teats easily. After a few weeks of kidding, the doe will have some bloody discharge. To reduce the build-up of this, you must keep the tail area clean.
- You must also stop milking the goat during the last two months of pregnancy. This helps her prepare the body for pregnancy and allows her to use all the energy for kidding.

You will also need a kidding pen or shelter. This should be ready before 145 days of pregnancy. The pen must have a bedding of clean wool. The walls must be sanitized using bleach water. A chunk of fresh straw must be placed there. You will also need a clean bucket for water when the kidding process begins.

It is also recommended that you put a basic kidding kit together so that you are not scampering for things during the birth. Here are the things you will need:

- 7% iodine to dip the umbilical cord
- A can to hold the iodine
- A flashlight
- The phone number of your vet or your goat care advisor
- Dental floss to tie the umbilical cord before you cut it
- Bulb suction to make sure that the airway and nostrils of the kid are clear.
- Old towels

- Betadine surgical scrub. In case the goat needs assistance, you must wash your hands and the goat with this.
- Sterilized surgical scissors to cut the cord
- KY jelly to ease the delivery
- Disposable gloves
- Feed bags
- Feeding syringe or tube for any weak kid
- Empty feeding bottle.

With all this in hand, the only thing to do is wait for the auspicious moment.

5. Is your goat ready for kidding?

The next thing you need to pay attention to is when the doe is ready for kidding. There are some obvious signs that you need to look for when your doe approaches the end of the gestation period.

Check the ligaments

Typically, the rump of a goat is solid and straight. However, when it comes to a doe that is approaching the end of a gestation period, you will notice a marked difference. You will see that her tail bone is elevated. In addition to that, the ligaments between the pelvis and the tailbone begin to loosen and stretch. This is her way of preparing for the kid that is on its way. Sometimes, you will notice a hollow on either sides of the tail. This is a sure sign that kidding will begin.

The best way to check if your doe is ready for kidding is to gently feel the ligaments that are present on either sides of the tail. In a doe that is not pregnant, these ligaments are rather firm. On the other hand, when the goat is ready for kidding, this part will become a lot more limp and soft.

When the ligaments are soft, it is a sign that kidding will take place in the next 24 hours. Sometimes, you might just read the signs wrong and put out a false alarm. But, over time, you will be able to tell exactly when the kid will be born.

You can start a routine check of the ligaments just a few weeks before kidding. When you see that they have become mushy, the doe is ready for kidding.

There are other signs that you can look or as well. They include:

- Standing away from the crowd or looking spaced out

- Discharge of white or yellow mucus near the vulva

- A bagged up udder that looks shiny and firm

- Change in behavior which may range from aggression to over friendliness.

- Restlessness. She will paw the ground, get up and sit and just look very uncomfortable.

When you are sure that the goat is ready to kid, keep your kit handy and make sure that you shift the doe to the kidding pen. If it is your first kidding, you may want to look for some assistance.

6. Dealing with labor

Goats seldom require the assistance of human beings when they are in labor. All you need to do is make arrangements for the birth and the goat will be able to get through labor on her own. However, it is useful for every goat owner to know a few basic things about labor.

Labor in goats occurs in two stages. The two stages of labor are as follows.

The first stage

This is when the uterus contracts and dilates. The mother is actually forcing the kid out through the cervix. This stage of labor lasts for almost 12 hours if this is your goat's first time kidding.

117

The first stage differs as per the breed of the goat and the age of the goat.

The goat will be extremely restless at this time. She will look from side to side almost as if she does not know what is going on. She may try to lick you sometimes. However, goats like to be alone during this time. It is also a common observation that the labor slows down or even comes to a halt if there are too many people around.

The second stage

During this stage, the babies are ready to come out of the birthing canal. The contractions become stronger and the baby is lined in the uterus appropriately. Then, it will start to make its way towards the birthing canal.

This stage lasts for just thirty minutes. So from the time the goat begins to push, until the time the baby is actually born, it will be less than half an hour. In case it takes longer, it could be the indication of a problem or some wrong positioning of the kid. You need to put your gloves on and investigate. If the baby is stuck or if there is some complication, you or your vet will have to intervene.

Then, you will notice the discharge getting thicker. It will also have traces of blood. There will also be a bubble at the vaginal opening. This is a sign that the amniotic membrane is coming out. When you look closely at this bubble, you will see the nose or the hooves of the little one.

Now the goat will continue to push the kid out. She may stop a couple of times to gather some strength. She may show other signs of fatigue such as walking in circles, try to nip at the bubble, or lick your hands thinking that it is a baby. When the kids are out, they may be in the amniotic membrane sometimes.

It is common for the kids to be born back first. This is not really a complication although the kid may inhale the amniotic fluid at times. If you notice a breech birth, you may have to pull the hind legs out to make sure that the head comes out easily.

Swinging the kid

This is necessary if the kid has had a breeched birth or back birth. That is when you need to remove any fluid that they may have snorted in by mistake. You must follow these steps to swing the kid:

- Wrap the kid with a towel

- With one hand, hold the feet of the kid. With the other hand, hold the area between the neck and head.

- You must swing the kid back and forth keeping the head out. This will clear the lungs. Be careful as the kid is slippery.

- If the kid is not breathing, repeat this process.

If the baby is born with the front legs back, you will need veterinary assistance. You will notice the nose of the baby but no hooves. This means that the legs are turned in, stalling the birth. You may also need assistance if the baby is placed across the cervix, the head is to one side and the head comes out first. In worst cases, a caesarean may be performed.

7. Caring for the mother and kid

Once the kid is born, you need to provide immediate care to the mother and the kid. As soon as the labor ends, take some warm water with some molasses to the mother. This will give her energy. You must then give her some alfalfa and grains. She can munch on this while the kids try to walk or nurse. In the meantime you need to wait for the placenta.

This is considered the third stage of labor. It is when the placenta comes out. It may take up to 12 hours for this process to get completed. Sometimes, it may even pass within an hour or two.

You must dispose this placenta immediately or burn it as it may contain harmful parasites.

Like most mammals, does may also try to eat the placenta. You may allow her to take a few bites as long as she does not choke on it.

The next step is to clean the kidding area. You need to remove all the soaked straws and replace with fresh straw. In case you want to feed the babies using a bottle, milk the doe completely. You can even treat the colostrum before you feed it. It is a good idea to freeze it in case of an emergency.

As soon as the kids are born, they may not appreciate the idea of being handled. However, you need to make sure that they are warm and stimulated enough to get on their feet. Once the new born has arrived, you have to do the following.

- Clean the kid using a towel. You must start with the head to check if the kid is breathing. If you don't notice breathing, rub the body or swing him. If you plan to bottle feed the kid, you need to clean it before the doe cleans him. Then you must wash him and place him in a separate box.

- The umbilical cord must be tied using dental floss. You must cut it just an inch away from the kid's body.

- Dip the cord in iodine. You must coat the whole cord. Using iodine prevents infections.

- Check the kid thoroughly for the gender and the see if there are any abnormalities.

- If the kid is going to be raised by the doe, put him under the doe for feeding. If the kid does not latch on or is unable to suckle, you may have to tube feed him. You must allow him to take his time. If you are bottle feeding the kid, offer a bottle with warm colostrum immediately. To warm the colostrum, place it in a water jar or 135 degrees Fahrenheit for about an hour. The temperature of the colostrum must be under 130 degrees.

8. Care for a goat that is nursing

The first thing that you need to do with a goat that is nursing is prevent mastitis. This means that you must follow the following udder care practises:

- A routine must be followed to milk the goat to prevent overfilling or injury.

- The udder and the teats must be washed and dried before milking to prevent bacterial infection.

- The teats must be sanitized after milking.

- Food must be available for the goat after milking so that it stands until the teat canal closes.

- Caring for any injury of the udder.

We will discuss prevention and treatment of mastitis in the following chapters. One important preventive measure is drying the doe off. This is when you plan to take a break from the milking routine. You must start by reducing the milking routine to just once a day. Then you will have to stop milking altogether.

Of course, you cannot just stop at will. Your doe must be ready to stop, too. If it is winter and if she has been milking for several months, you must wait and be patient. When you start drying the doe off, her udder may swell because of the accumulation of milk. You must not milk her at this time to prevent mastitis.

In case you are drying off a doe that already has mastitis, you must use a recommended intramammary antibiotic.

9. Creating a milking routine

Goats simply love routines. If you plan to milk your goat, you must make sure that you have a set routine to get maximum milk each time. This will also ease the process of milking. You must use the same place and the same methods every day. A milking routine includes:

- A special area for milking so that the goat is not disturbed by other members of the herd.

- Sitting on the same side of the goat each time
.

- Washing the udder before starting the milking routine so that the udder is relaxed.

- Milking the goats in the exact order each day. You may change this order if one of the goats has mastitis or if she has just had a kid.

It is possible to milk a dam about three times a day. However, it consumes a lot of time and is not cost effective at all. The recommended practice is milking twice a day.

Hand milking a goat

Hand milking is the safest way to milk a goat. However, if you have a condition such as carpel tunnel or if you are uncomfortable milking a goat, you could opt for machine milking. Hand milking a goat includes the following steps:

- Secure the goat to a milk stand and place some grain to distract her.

- Wash your hands thoroughly

- Wash the udder and teats and sanitize them with special teat wipes. Then dry them with a paper towel.
- Now wrap the fingers and the thumb around one teat and trap some milk in the teat. Once the milk is trapped milk it out quickly to get two squirts into a cup from each teat. This lets you check for any abnormality in the milk

- When you are convinced about the quality of the milk, you can milk into a clean stainless steel bucket. Never pull the teats to hard.

- Once the teat is empty, massage it and bump it with your fists gently.

- Filter the milk

- Spray the teats with a sept teat dip

- Allow the goat to return to the herd

- Make sure you clean the bucket thoroughly.

In case you plan to have dam raise kids, you must allow them to feed as they wish for the first two weeks. Then, you must separate the kid and the dam. The dam must be milked every morning before letting her out. On the other hand, if the kid is bottle raised, the dam must be milked immediately.

If the goat needs to be prepared for two milking sessions each day, you will have to follow this routine twice, whether you milk the goat in the evening or not. That way, you can help them wean the kids and be milked twice each day.

Chapter 13: Health And Well Being

The health of your Fainting Goat is your responsibility. If you are unable to take good care of your pets, they may become infected or may even die. The most difficult thing with diseases related to animals like the goat is that they spread to the entire herd even before you can notice it. So, you must be vigilant and watch out for some obvious signs that will tell you that your goat is unwell.

The good thing about goats is that they have very unique characteristics and behavior patterns. Any deviation from normalcy is a sign that your goat is either unwell, or is stressed for various reasons. There are some common symptoms that you must look out for if you suspect that your goat has fallen sick:

Not chewing cud: Also known as ruminating, this is a habit that is displayed always among goats. This is a part of the digestion process. If your goat is healthy, he will ruminate as soon as he eats. If the goat does not do this, it is a clear indication that there is some problem with his digestive tract.

Difficulty in walking: If your goat is limping, it is an indication that he is either suffering from injury in the hoof or that he has developed some knee problem. If your goat staggers, you need to be alert for neurological problems.

Head pressing and teeth grinding: They are both signs of pain among goats. You will have to investigate if this problem persists.

Altered breathing pace: If your goat displays labored breathing or slow breathing, you need to worry about it. Sometimes, even too much heat may lead to labored breathing in goats.

Runny nose and eyes: These symptoms are indicative of some infection. They are also accompanied by coughing sometimes.

Abnormal droppings: If the poop of your goat is brownish and pelleted, it is a sign of some health problem. Even the consistency of the dropping is an indication of health.

What to do if you see these signs

There are some immediate measures that you can take when your goat shows these symptoms.
- Take the temperature of the goat
- Check if there are any ruminations
- Check the heart rate
- Check for injuries
- Check for crusty eyes
- Pinch the skin on the neck and see it is comes back to the normal position immediately. If the skin gathers into a tent and returns to normal very slowly, it is an indication of dehydration.

You must make a note of all these things and take them with you when you visit the vet to help the diagnosis.

1. Common diseases in goats

Enterotoxemia Type C

This is a disease of the digestive tract that is seen in two forms. In the adult goats, it is called struck and in kids, it is called enterotoxic hemorrahgic enteritis.

This disease is observed in kids after a few days of birth.

Symptoms
- **In adults:** Ulcerations of the small intestine
- **In kids:** Bloody Diarrhea
- Death, without any symptoms
- Swelling of the face

Causes
- Indigestion
- Overabundance of milk for the kids

Prevention
- Parturition under hygienic conditions
- Cleaning the udders regularly
- Eliminating dung from the shelter
- Eliminating dirt rags

Treatment
- No successful treatment method yet.

Pulpy Kidney or Enterotoxemia Type D

This condition occurs in young that are less that 3 weeks old.

Symptoms
- Limber neck with reduced muscular control
- Loss of Muscular control in limbs
- Convolutions

Causes
- Weaning in feedlots
- High Carbohydrate diets
- Sudden change in feed

Tetanus or lockjaw

Symptoms
- Rigidness
- Muscle spasms
- Death

Causes
- Entry of bacteria *Clostridium tetani* into the body.
- Secondary to procedures like castrations

Treatment
- Preventive care only
- Vaccination
- Good hygiene

Tips: *Tetanus can spread to human beings so be careful when you are handling an infected goat.*

Soremouth

This disease is also called ecthyma. It is a viral disease of the skin. This condition is more prominent in lactating does when they have not been vaccinated.

It is caused by the Pox virus. The animals may come in contact with other infected animals, feed of these animals or even bedding that has been exposed to this virus.

Symptoms
- Slow rate of growth
- Loss of condition
- Reduced immunity
- No willingness to eat
- **In does:** Premature weaning and mastitis

Treatment
- Allow them to clear out on their own
- Spray recommended insecticide to ward of flies
- Vaccination

Tips: *The soremouth virus can spread to human beings so be careful when you are handling an infected goat.*

Pneunomonia

This is a serious condition among goats and there are several types of pneumonia that can affect them. So, once you identify the condition, make sure you check with your vet for the most effective treatment

Symptoms
- Temperature above 104 degrees Fahrenheit
- Anorexia
- Depression
- Difficulty in breathing

Causes
- Viral or bacterial infection
- Change of weather
- Poor quality of air
- Transport
- Weaning

Treatment
Once diagnosed, antibiotics are administered for pneumonia

Prevention
- Optimum sanitation
- Use air purifiers
- Good ventilation
- Quarantining new goats
- Good nutrition
- Reduction of transportation costs

Foot rot

This condition is mostly prevalent in areas that are warm and moist. The symptoms vary as per the degree of infection and also as per the strain of bacteria that has infected the foot.

Symptoms
- Redness and inflammation between toes
- Bad odor
- Hoof horn separates from the hoof
- Lameness
- Reduced food consumption as animals will not go to the feed
- Reduced reproductive abilities.

Causes
- Infection by *Fusobacterium necrophorum* and *Dichelobacter nodosus.*
- Viral infection

Treatment
- Good Husbandry
- Antibiotics
- Vaccination

Prevention
- Quarantining
- Regular hoof trimming

Caseous Lymphadenitis

This condition affects the lymphatic system and results in several abscesses in the nodes and in the internal organs of the goat. When it reaches the internal system, it may be fatal to the animal.

Symptoms
- Visible abscesses
- Anorexia
- Weight loss
- Fever

Causes
- Infection by *Corynebacterium pseudotuberculosis*
- Contact with other infected animals

- Contaminated environment

Treatment
- Antibiotics
- Vaccination

Prevention
- Quarantining
- Good husbandry

Listerosis

Symptoms
- Anorexia
- Depression
- Salivating excessively
- Paralysis of the face
- Involuntary running
- Falling to the sides

Cause
- Infection by *bacteria Listeria monocytogenes*

Treatment
- Isolating the animals
- Testing the cerebrospinal fluid
- High penicillin doses
- Supported by insulin and fluids

Prevention
- Healthy feeding conditions

Polioencephalomacia

This condition affects young feedlot goats that are between the ages of 5 to 8 months.

Symptoms

- Lack of coordination
- Weakness
- Tremors
- Blindness
- Depression
- Seizures
- Muscular contractions

Causes
- Thyamine deficiency
- High level of sulphur in the food

Treatment
- Isolation
- Intravenous fluids
- Electrolytes
- Nutrients

Prevention
- Highly nutritious diet
- Reduction in sulphur content of the food

Mastitis

This condition affects the mammary glands of does.

Symptoms
- Swollen udders
- Warmness in udders
- Pain in the udder
- Different consistency of the milk
- Anorexia
- Depression
- Fever
- Lethargy
- Death of offspring

Cause
- Bacterial infection of the mammary glands

Treatment
- Intramammary antibiotics
- Systemic antibiotics
- Surgery

Prevention
- High sanitation
- Recommended mastitis control strategy that you can get from your vet

White Muscle Disease

This is a degenerative disease that mainly affects the muscles along with the skeletal muscles and the heart muscles

Symptoms
- Low conception rate
- Reduced quality of milk
- Reduced immunity
- Reduced quality of the semen
- Placenta retention

Causes
- Infection by bacteria
- Vitamin E deficiency
- Selenium deficiency

Treatment
- Culturing the causative agent and administering antibiotics accordingly.
- Vitamin E and selenium injection

Prevention
- High quality feed
- Supplementation

Pregnancy Toxemia

This condition occurs during the late stage of gestation. It occurs in animals that are carrying multiple feti.

Symptoms

- Ketosis
- Depression
- Weakness and Fatigue

Causes
- Insufficient nutrition
- Obesity
- Underweight goats

Treatment
- Nutrient dense fodder

Prevention
- High quality feed
- Managing weight of the does
- Feeding energy rich foods during the trimester

Lactic Acidosis or Grain Overload

Symptoms
- Fever
- Weakness
- Lethargy
- Muscle twitching
- Teeth grinding
- Diarrhea

Causes
- High carbohydrate intake
- Lowering of pH in the ruminal region
- Inability to metabolise lactic acid

Treatment
- Feeding the animals dietary buffers like calcium carbonate

Prevention
- Introducing high grain diets slowly
- Reducing starch consumption

Copper Toxicity

Sheep and goats are very sensitive to the copper content in their food. The problem with this condition is that it develops over time. The copper accumulates in the liver and the animal may die without any clinical symptoms.

Treatment
- Drenching the liver
- Feeding ammonium molybdate
- Penicillamine
- Sodium Sulfate

Prevention
- Testing the food for cooper level
- Feeding specially formulated foods
- Supplementing with molybdenum

2. Abortive Diseases

Any disease that causes the death of the offspring before it is born is called an abortive disease. In some cases, abortive diseases may also refer to the birth of a deformed baby or a very weak baby.

There are two types of abortion: infectious and non infectious abortion. The non infectious abortion is mostly due to trauma that can be caused during fighting or accidents. These are less common.

Usually abortions in goats are caused by vibriosis, salmonella, chlamydia, listeria and cache valley virus.

When you are handling the aborted foetus, you must take several preventive measures as the pathogens are easily transmitted to human beings.

Here are some types of abortive diseases that you must watch out for:

Campylobacter infections: These infections can lead to delayed pregnancy and also still births. The best treatment of infection by *campylobacter* strain of bacteria is sulfa drugs or tetracycline. There are several vaccines that you can give your goat to prevent this condition.

Chlamydia: This causes abortions in the last few weeks of gestation. It usually results in stillbirth and sometimes weak offspring. The problem with chlamydia is that the infecting agent is shed from the reproductive tract, spreading the infection to the rest of the herd. Even when Chlamydia tetracycline shots have been successful. You may also add tetracycline in the feed. Vaccinations to prevent chlamydia are available.

Taxoplasmosis: If the doe suffers from taxoplasmosis in the early stages of gestation, the foetus may be reabsorbed. Only when the infection occurs in the later stages does taxoplasmosis cause deaths or abortions. The difference in this type of infection is that the agent is not a bacterium but a protozoan parasite.

These parasites are commonly seen in rodents and cats. They tend to shed these parasites in their droppings. If it is accidentally consumed by the goat, infection may occur. There is no treatment for this condition. You can only take preventive measures.

You must always make sure that the food is properly covered. Stray cats must not be allowed near the shelter if there are pregnant does. You can give your goat a coccidiostat such as Decoquinate. When you are giving a goat coccidiostats, make sure they are FDA approved.

Leptospirosis: This is caused by the bacteria *Leptospira interrogans.* When the animal comes in contact with still water, this infection may be contracted. The most common symptoms of this condition are anemia and icterus. Icterus is commonly known as jaundice. The dam's placenta, urine and absorbed foetus can be tested to diagnose the condition.

Q Fever: This is a bacterial infection that is common in goats. It is caused by the bacteria *Coxiella burnetti.* This bacteria is shed in the urine, faeces, milk, placental tissue and is also transmitted through the air. This condition results in lesions, anorexia and abortion. You can manage an outbreak with the help of tetracycline. You must also isolate the animal. Any reproductive waste that is produced must be burnt or buried to prevent infections in the rest of the herd.

Whenever you notice any abortive disease in a doe, you must take preventive measures immediately. Your vet will be able to help you diagnose the condition quite easily. The best way to find out what the exact disease is, is to submit the placenta or the absorbed foetus to a diagnostic clinic.

You must make sure that the part of the placenta that has lesions. It is also a good idea to isolate any pregnant doe from the rest of the herd to ensure that the herd does not get infected.

3. Parasites

Parasites can cause extensive damage to animals like goats. They are one of the most common health threats for goats. If there is a parasitic infection in the goat, the damage may be caused by several aspects of your goat's wellbeing. The gastrointestinal tract can be damaged, the rate of growth reduces, the quality of meat, milk and fibre reduces and reproduction is compromised. In severe cases, parasitic infections can be fatal to the animal.

There are some clinical signs of parasitic infections that you must look out for. The most common symptoms include:

- Sudden weight gain or loss
- Reduced reproductive abilities
- Diarrhea
- Lack of thriftness
- Loss of appetite

There are several factors that make an animal susceptible to parasitic infections. These factors include the basic genetic make up of the animal, the age and the reproductive stage that the animal is in.

Parasites are common to animals like goat and sheep. However, with goats, there is an increased threat of internal parasitic infection. Young goats, lactating does and pregnant does are most susceptible to parasitic infections.

Internal parasites

There are various types of internal parasites that can affect goats. Usually, there is some natural parasitic activity that occurs in the body of the goat. While that is normal, an excessive presence of internal parasites can be damaging to the goat's health and also fatal in severe cases.

In goats, the most common internal parasite is the roundworm. This parasite naturally lives in the small intestine and the abomasum of goats. There are various strains of roundworms that can cause infections, including *Telodorsagia circumcinta, Trichostrongylus colubriformis and Haemonchus contortus.*

The last one mentioned above is the most dangerous internal parasite. It is also called the baber pole worm. This is a blood sucking parasite that can lay several eggs within the body of the animal. If your goat has been affected by *Haemonchus contortus,* the signs that you will observe include lethargy, weakness, edema and swelling of the lower jaw. This condition is also called bottle jaw.

Tapeworms

These parasites can cause gastrointestinal problems and weight loss. If you observe yellowish or white segments in the faeces of the goats, you can be sure that it is a tapeworm infection. Usually tapeworm infections occur when the animal is about 4 to 5 months old. Usually after this age, kids will develop resistance towards tapeworms.

The problem with tapeworms is that they are overrated. When owners see these segments in the faeces, they just begin to treat the animal for tapeworms. However, there could be several other parasites that are extremely deadly for the animal. So, you must make sure that your goat gets the attention of a veterinarian when you notice the common symptoms for a tapeworm infection.

Coccidia

This is a protozoan parasite that can affect the small intestine in goats. The small intestine is susceptible to parasitic infections because it is the most important site for nutrient absorption. The most common signs of coccidia infection are stunted growth, anemia, hair breakage, dehydration, fever and diarrhea with blood and mucous.

This condition is mostly prevalent in animals that are raised in confinement. It is caused due to poor sanitation, lack of clean water and overcrowding. You can control coccidian infections by rotating the pastures, limiting the number of goats in one shelter, sanitation techniques and providing clean drinking water. You may also include FDA approved coccidiostats in the food of your goats.

It is possible to treat an outbreak with sulfa drugs.

External parasites
External parasites mainly damage the fleece of the goats leading to reduced value of the animal. The most common external

parasites are mites, lice, keds etc. The occurrence of external parasites is higher during the colder months, especially if the shelter of the goats is overcrowded.

There are several species of lice that you may find on goats. They are broadly categorised as chewing and sucking lice. The chewing lice simply feed on the dead skin cells. On the other hand, the sucking lice feed on the blood. You will notice eggs or nits on the hair of the goat. Also, hair loss is common when your goat has lice. You can use topical insecticides for the chewing lice and anthlemintics for the sucking lice.

Keds are a little more dangerous. They can actually pierce the skin to suck blood. They will be found on the flanks, the shoulders and the neck. The bites of keds are very irritating to goats. You will see signs like persistent scratching and gnawing. This damages the wool. You can shear the goat to remove the larve. You can also use insecticides and ivermectin injections to wipe out an infestation. Mites are hard to notice as they live beneath the skin. This irritates the goats and makes them scratch themselves. The itching is so severe that it may lead to scabs and wounds. You can use topical insecticides and ivermectin injections to prevent this infection.

4. Common vaccinations for goats

Vaccinating your goat is the best, and the most effective preventive measure against most diseases. If you are running a business with goats, it is especially important to vaccinate the animal to make your business more sustainable.

At the minimum, you must vaccinate your goat against *clostridium perfringens and tetanus.* However, most goat owners neglect this important part of goat care.

You must vaccinate your goat because:

- Deadly diseases may be prevented

- In case of any infection despite the vaccination, it is less severe and is shorter.
- Death is preventable if your goat is vaccinated.
- It's cheaper than replacing a goat or having a mass outbreak in your herd.

Here are some common vaccinations recommended for goats

Vaccination	Disease Prevented	When to Vaccinate
CDT	Entrotoxemia and Tentanus	Fourth month in case of does, after 1 month in kids. You must give all your goats and annual booster shot
CLA	Cornybacterium pseudotuberculosis	One shot when kids are 3 months old. Second shot three week later and an annual booster
Pneumonia	Pasteurella multocida or Mannheimia Haemolytica pneumonia	Two doses that are 2 or 3 weeks apart
Chlamydia	Chlamydia abortion	First 28 to 45 days after pregnancy
Rabies	Rabies	Annually
Soremouth	Soremouth	Annually

5. Finding a Good Goat Veterinarian

Unfortunately, the veterinarian you take your dog or cat to may not be qualified to treat your goats. Fortunately, finding a veterinarian who specializes in farm animals or goats is not as hard to find as it was years ago.

To find a veterinarian, begin by asking the breeder, retailer or individual from whom you purchased the goats. Often, they will have a relationship with a veterinarian accustomed to caring for farm animals. If that does not work, you can ask other goat hobbyists in your area.

If none of these strategies allows you to locate a vet, search the Internet and local phone listings. If possible, search for reviews of the veterinarian before visiting him or her.

Remember that goats are not dogs or cats, and a trip to the veterinarian can be an especially stressful event. Therefore, a veterinarian that makes house calls is especially helpful. However, your goats may require hospitalization or surgery to remedy some illnesses, so it is important that the veterinarian has access to a place suitable for such procedures.

Always locate and meet with your veterinarian soon after acquiring your herd. This way, you can become acquainted with the vet if you are not already, and your vet can give your goats a preliminary physical to ensure they are healthy.

One of the other reasons to visit your veterinarian immediately after acquiring your goats is to prevent the spread of any diseases they have to their new environment.

For example, if your newly purchased goats have an illness, and you take them directly from the breeder to your home, they may spread the disease throughout their enclosure.

Later, when you take them to the veterinarian and have them treated, you must then take them back to their enclosure, where they will become re-infected, thus necessitating further treatment.

Additionally, you will be forced to clean the entire enclosure – including the water reservoir – from top to bottom.

Therefore, if at all possible, take the goats directly from the place you acquire them to the veterinarian's office.

6. Guidelines to Help Prevent Disease

It is impossible to eliminate the potential for disease transmission. However, by following these three guidelines, you can greatly reduce the risks to your pets, and give them a better chance at living long, healthy lives:

- Minimize the stress on your goats, so that their immune systems operate at peak efficiency.

- Do not let your goats socialize. Keep your goats away from all other animals like dogs or cats

- Immunize the goats against as many diseases as possible.

By examining the ways in which different diseases can infect goats, the reasons for these three guidelines are clear.

In broad terms, some infectious agents are ubiquitous, and only cause problems when they overwhelm an animal's immune system. This is most likely to occur in stressed animals that do not have access to proper housing, or are fed improper diets. Coccidiosis is one example of this type of pathogen. It infects most goats, but usually only causes symptoms when a particularly lethal strain is ingested, or when the goats ingest large quantities of the sporulated oocysts (the infectious particles for these parasitic protozoans) (Larry R. McDougald, 2012).

Accordingly, it is important to provide your goat with a clean habitat, feed them the most nutritious diet possible, and ensure that they are protected from inclement weather and temperature extremes, to avoid these types of pathogens, and the illnesses they cause.

Other infectious agents may pass from one host to another, and are not likely to infect goats that do not come into contact with other goats. For example, a goat housed singly for the entirety of his life, who does not share water or space with other goats, is unlikely to develop Caseous Lymphadenitis. However, a goat only needs to sip infected water once to become infected, and ultimately die. Your herd will undoubtedly exchange germs amongst themselves, so you must effectively quarantine your herd. Try to purchase goats from the same breeder or retailer, and avoid adding other members to the herd at a later time.

Take care to prevent wild animals from sharing a water source with your herd. Additionally, be careful when visiting other places with goats; a frequent way diseases are spread is via dirt particles that cling to people's shoes or clothing. Ensure that visitors have not recently been around other goats.

Therefore, as explained in the first two guidelines, you should provide your goats with the very best care possible, to ensure that your goat's immune system is working as well as it can and that they do not share water, space or the company of other goats.

Immunization is the process of injecting a dead, weakened or sub-infectious quantity of a virus into a potential host before it gets sick. When this occurs, the goat's immune systems learn to fight off this virus, while not being at risk of becoming sick. This way, when the goats eventually encounter the live virus, their immune systems defeat it, keeping them from getting sick.

Some vaccines provide lifetime immunity, while others must be given repeatedly to remain effective.

By following these three guidelines, you are likely to reduce the chances of illness in your flock significantly.

Emergency and First Aid

If you notice injuries or sudden health problems in your goat, choking for instance, you must be able to provide them with first aid. A well-equipped first aid kit is the first step towards ensuring immediate help for your goats. The must haves in your First Aid Kit are:

Tweezers: Splinters are a common problem in goats. If these splinters are not removed correctly, they will bleed profusely. So it is recommended that you remove them tweezers.

Blood Coagulant: Injuries or cuts might cause profuse bleeding. It is good to have a blood coagulant to help take care of this issue.

Bag Balm: This is a petroleum based products that can be used to soothe wounds and sores.

Eye Ointment: When goats get into fights, they are most often prone to eye injuries. Having an antibacterial eye ointment can prevent severe infections.

Syringes or droppers: In some conditions, you might have to drop water or oil directly into the throat of the goat. Syringes and droppers can be used for this. They are also handy when you have to give baby goats oral medication.

Rubber gloves: Handling goats with injuries and infection puts you at the risk of infections. Using rubber gloves will keep you safe.

Now that you have all the information you need on healthcare of goats, you can rest assured that you will be able to maintain your herd well.

7. Getting Insurance

Getting a pet insurance is equivalent to getting any sort of insurance, be it your own health insurance or car insurance. In some cases, pet insurance is mandatory to get your goat the license that is necessary to have him in the house legally. The idea is to get your goat's health insured so that he can get the right attention when necessary. There are several factors that determine the type of insurance policy that you will get. The premium that you pay on your insurance depends on three things:

• The age of your goat- the older your goat the higher will the premium be.

• The breed of your goat- the premium that you pay for goats of a purer breed is higher as these goats require expensive care and treatment.

• The type of coverage that you require- You must be sure of what you want your policy to cover. The coverage sum is also an important factor for your premium.

With most insurance policies, you should be able to get coverage for injuries due to accidents, common medical problems, poisoning and even severe terminal diseases like cancer. There are some policies that will also cover things like immunization, routine care, flea control prescription, annual checkups and also dental care. Of course these policies are quite expensive and require a higher premium payment.

When you consider the costs of going to the vet and getting your goat checked up thoroughly, you will realize that getting insurance is a great thing to do. In an untoward situation when your pet requires attention, you will be able to provide him with all the necessary care and attention without making any compromises. Insurance is especially necessary when you are trying to raise a herd for business.

Most pet owners neglect this rather important step towards pet care. In my personal experience, I have seen that the anxiety and the sorrow that the owners go through in case of medical emergencies is quite traumatic. So, I recommend that you speak to your breeder or even an insurance agent to get the right information about the policies that are available in the market. The best people to give you accurate advice are people who already have pet insurances for their little ones. They will be able to tell you why a certain policy will work and why another will fail.

Pet insurance coverage can cost anywhere from $2,000 to $6,000 USD (£1201 to £3604) over an average lifespan of a goat, and unless your goat is involved in a serious accident, or contracts a life-threatening disease, you may never need to pay out that much for treatment.

Conclusion

Now that you are equipped with all the information that you need with respect to the Fainting Goats, I am sure that you will make a great owner. It is a lot of work to keep goats at home. While that may sound intimidating, if you are unable to match all the requirements and needs of your pets, you will only compromise on their health and well-being. To conclude, I would like to remind you that a goat is a big financial commitment.

Here is a breakdown of the approximate costs of keeping a Fainting Goat:

- Price of the goat: $75to $300 or £50 to £150
- Health Certificate: $40 to $50 or £20 to £25
- Fencing: $2500 to $1000 or £1500 to £6000
- Enclosures: $300 to $600 or £150 to £300
- Bedding: $10 or £6 per goat per month
- Feed: $7 to $10 or £5 to £10 for a 40 pound bag
- Feeder: $3 to $10 or £5 to £10
- Waterer: $3 to $20 or £5 to £10
- Annual Vet cost: $150 to $500 or £80 to £250
- Hoof trimmers: $20 or £10
- Deworming medication: $15 or £7 every four months

Once you are sure of making this commitment, you can convert your home into a great place for your Fainting Goats.

I hope this book answers all your questions about having Fainting Goats.

CPSIA information can be obtained
at www.ICGtesting.com
Printed in the USA
BVOW06s1002270117
474656BV00013B/271/P